Dear Diary, I'm Pregnant

TEENAGERS TALK ABOUT THEIR PREGNANCY

Interviews by Anrenée Englander

Edited by Corinne Morgan Wilks

Annick Press • Toronto • New York

Annick Press Ltd.

Annick Press gratefully acknowledges the support of the
Canada Council and the Ontario Arts Council.

Cataloguing in Publication Data
  Main entry under title:
  Dear diary, I'm pregnant : teenagers talk about their pregnancy

  ISBN 1-55037-440-0

  1. Teenage pregnancy.   2. Pregnant schoolgirls - Interviews.
  I. Englander, Anrenée. II. Wilks, Corinne Morgan.
  III. Title.

  HQ759.4.D42 1997   306.874'3'0922   C97-930222-6

Distributed in Canada by:
Firefly Books Ltd.
66 Leek Crescent,
Richmond Hill, ON
L4B 1H1

Published in the U.S.A.
by Annick Press (U.S.) Ltd.
Distributed in the U.S.A. by:
Firefly Books (U.S.) Inc.
P.O. Box 1338
Ellicott Station
Buffalo, NY 14205

Printed and bound in Canada by Webcom.

Contents

To those I owe so much...
Mom, for teaching me about choice and for being so proud of me
Karen, for always showing me what's right and
Warren, for knowing who I am, and loving me anyway
— A.E.

Preface

This book is about choice. A young woman confronted with an unplanned pregnancy might feel overwhelmed, scared, even suicidal. *Dear Diary, I'm Pregnant* allows teenagers the opportunity to "meet" other teenagers who have had to confront this situation and to see how they handled that experience.

I developed the premise for this book in 1991, when a young woman I knew found herself facing an unplanned pregnancy. Wishing to help her, I looked for a book that offered information on her choices and what she might expect from each one. That book did not exist. In the next few years, two more young women I knew experienced that same situation. Feeling as helpless as I had in the past, I decided to try to develop the book myself. I began my research and approached Annick Press with my idea in 1994.

Over the next two years, I distributed flyers all over North America asking teenage girls who had been pregnant to come forward and be interviewed. The flyers were posted in health clinics, hospitals, high schools, shelters and anywhere else I might reach pregnant teens. Knowing my readers would come from all walks of life, my aim was to interview teenagers from many cultures, races and socio-economic backgrounds. Ultimately, I spoke with nearly forty young women. The interviews were held in their homes or other places where they felt comfortable, and they usually lasted three hours.

During the interviews, the teens would discuss extremely painful issues, which often brought them to tears. At those times I felt that I was exploiting them. I knew, though, that the interviews should continue, because by communicating these details these teens would help others to make decisions about their own pregnancies.

It should be acknowledged that one scenario was not encountered in any of the interviews: a young woman decides to keep her child and finds subsequently that this decision has led to extreme hardship or unhappiness. While the teens in this book discuss some of the burdens of being a mother, they always go on to describe the pleasures. Some teens never feel the rewards of motherhood, however; none of these women came forward to be interviewed for this book. It is very difficult for a teenage mother to admit to herself and to society that she made the wrong choice in keeping her baby, but that reality does exist and must be recognized.

I have to believe that the stories were told to me in good faith. (The reader must also take into consideration that I heard only one side of each multifaceted story.) At times, however, the possibility was triggered in my mind that I was being lied to. Nevertheless, as I was not investigating but merely reporting, I have to trust that these women were being honest with me and with themselves, and that they were motivated only by their hope of helping another teen.

This book is not meant to be a platform for advocating one choice over another. On the contrary, we—the Interviewer, the Editor and the Publisher—came to this project hoping to broaden the spectrum of ideas for our readers. Although not all the stories have a happy ending or even a clear resolution, each one was carefully selected so that there would be an overall balance between adoption, abortion and motherhood. We also worked to ensure that the interviews reflected a variety of responses, so as not to perpetuate or form any stereotypes in the reader's mind.

At the same time, we are aware of the fact that none of the young women interviewed would be classified as a "perfect daughter" coming from an "ideal family" (in which the parents are happily married, financially stable, and neither physically nor sexually abuse their children). But we know that teen pregnancy can and does happen through every strata of our society; nobody is exempt. Thus, it is very important for the reader to know that while "model teenagers" (for example, those who do not use drugs, are "A" students and have not left home) are seen by counsellors and agencies all the time, none responded to our requests to be interviewed.

In compiling *Dear Diary, I'm Pregnant*, I wanted to create a vehicle for pregnant teenagers to learn of the hopes and dreams, and even the darkest secrets, of other teens who have faced an unplanned pregnancy. I hope this book will make the decisions of a pregnant teen clearer, easier and much less frightening.

A final note: we have changed and/or concealed all names, places and clearly identifiable details in order to protect the privacy of the interviewees and their families.

Anrenée Englander
Toronto, Canada

Acknowledgements

I would like to express my deepest thanks to Warren Hales, Leah Erna Beck, Karen Englander, Bill McLaughlin and Tania Englander, who all tirelessly imparted their invaluable advice and offered their unwavering support every time I needed it, and even when I didn't. I love you.

I would also like to thank Rick Wilks, without whose faith and dedication there would not finally be a book, denying all of us who aided in its realization this opportunity to help so many others.

For their very great co-operation and assistance in encouraging teenagers to participate in the interviews, Helen Jones and her colleagues at the Morgentaler Clinic; Carolyn Kroeber, York Region Board of Education; Eileen Alexiou, Jessie's Centre; and Ruth Ewert, Evergreen Health Centre, thank you. My sincere appreciation to all the women and men in Canada and the United States who graciously took the time to return my phone calls and paste up our flyers.

Thank you to Corinne Morgan Wilks for devoting so much time and energy to editing the transcripts.

A special thank-you to Beth-Ann Little, who selflessly accepted that I pursue this endeavour alone.

I am especially indebted to all the young women who took the time to be interviewed. I am honoured to be the one to whom you chose to divulge your secrets, and touched that you were able to share your tears, your laughter and your truths with me. Whether or not your story lies within these pages, you have all helped somebody with their decision, as your story awarded me the guidance to ultimately make the best book that I could. Thank you.

Editor's Message

These stories are edited versions of substantially longer interviews. The contributors' words are as spoken in the interviews. The aim of the editing process was to preserve the young women's voices—their words, their flow and their idiomatic style of speaking—and to select and present their issues and concerns without bias or prejudice.

Corinne Morgan Wilks
Editor

Publisher's Message

Annick Press Ltd. does not advocate or endorse any course of action discussed in this publication. Furthermore, we caution the reader that it is impossible to reflect, in ten stories, the full range of experiences and situations faced by pregnant teens: teenagers from all segments of society can and do become pregnant, and each person's circumstances are unique.

We hope that this book will be a source of both emotional and psychological support for young people.

Annick Press Ltd.

"Except for memory, time would have no meaning at all."

Pat Conroy, *Beach Music*

Introduction

Teenage pregnancy is an important issue in several distinct ways. For teenagers themselves, pregnancy often comes as a shock and presents them with a number of difficult decisions, some of which will change their lives, and limited options; so, teenage pregnancy is certainly a significant personal problem. But teenage pregnancy has also been seen in recent years as a significant social problem, worthy of talk-show attention and even government action. The perception is that having large numbers of teen pregnancies is undesirable. It's hard to argue with this view; after all, who wishes to promote teenage pregnancy? Still, teenage pregnancy, while hardly a new phenomenon, did not always attract such attention as a social ill. When abortions were illegal, it was hard to know how many teenagers got them. It was also hard to know how many teenagers got married because they were pregnant; only "unwed mothers" were visible. Teenage pregnancy thus raises important questions about how social issues in general come to our attention and get defined as problems.

What do current statistics indicate about teenage pregnancy? That depends. Interpreting statistics requires making a variety of decisions. Are we interested simply in the *number* of teen pregnancies (which will go up when there are more teenagers) or in *rates* of teen pregnancy? Are we concerned about the issue of *pregnancies* in general, or about teen *births* and teen *mothers* in particular? Are we interested in *married* teenagers or only in *single* ones? And are we looking at all teenagers, up to the age of twenty, or only at those who are younger? And how much younger? Finally, when we examine trends, how long a time-frame shall we look at: broad trends over time, or only recent changes? As you can see, there are difficulties in providing a straightforward set of facts. Nevertheless, here is a very rough overview:

Over the past two decades, more young women have become sexually active and thus at risk of pregnancy. However, in many countries—including Canada—pregnancy rates have not risen, due to great public support for contraceptive use. By contrast, the pregnancy rates for young American women are high. In both countries, despite some variations over time, fewer teenagers are giving birth, due to the legalization and use of abortion. Among those who do give birth, many more are single, a fact that reflects the decline in the use of marriage as a "solution" to pregnancy. Moreover, teenagers who give birth to a child are even more likely now than in the past to keep the child rather than place it for adoption.

■

Over the past few years, researchers have begun to look more carefully and critically at many of the negative stereotypes and assumptions about teenage pregnancy and teen mothers.

One common myth is that teenagers get pregnant because they don't know about contraception. In reality, teenagers get pregnant for a variety of reasons, just as older women do. Many pregnancies occur in the first six months of sexual activity, or when teenagers discontinue contraceptive use between serious relationships out of concern for the possible health risks of the pill. Most teen pregnancies are accidental, and many happen in spite of contraceptive use, just as they do in older women. Most teenagers are knowledgeable about contraception, although they may not use it consistently. For some teenagers, sex education classes are an important source of information about birth control and the choices to consider when pregnant. However, in many schools contraception and abortion cannot be discussed. As well, access to abortion, birth-control resources and/or pregnancy counselling can vary enormously across Canada and the United States.

Once pregnant, teenagers face limited options, and most worry about how their boyfriends and families will react. Although teenage girls usually turn to their boyfriends and friends, and sometimes parents, for advice, they may keep their situation and their decision private for fear of disapproval. Thus, even though abortion is the most common option chosen (adoption is the least common), the public controversy around abortion has silenced girls from sharing their abortion experiences with one another, leaving each pregnant teenage girl or couple to face the decision on their own. Confronted by the reality of pregnancy, teenagers also find themselves re-evaluating their previous views in the light of their current circumstances. For example, our own research on teen mothers and the stories in this book show very clearly how a girl may reject the idea of an abortion for one pregnancy but accept it for a later one, or the reverse. Although we cannot assume that teenagers will or even should settle ahead of time on which option they *would* choose if they became pregnant, a more open discussion among teenagers about the options is useful.

Another common assumption about single teen mothers is that their boyfriends have abandoned them. One problem with this image, even when it is an accurate portrayal of the situation, is that it presents the teen mother as the victim of her boyfriend's decisions rather than as an agent with considerations of her own about the relationship. Several studies, including our own, suggest that young women may choose not to marry or live with boyfriends for a variety of reasons. Indeed, the experience of pregnancy itself may lead them to re-examine the relationship and the boyfriend's suitability as a partner and father. And even when teen mothers do not marry, they may live with or continue to be involved with boyfriends who support them in caring for their child, even if not financially.

Another common assumption is that teen mothers are inadequate mothers, either because they have chosen to have a child for the "wrong reasons" and will tire of motherhood, or because they lack the maturity and experience to care properly for a child. Yet some studies show that many teen mothers have had considerable child-care experience and can expect support from their own mothers in caring for their children. Findings like these have sometimes supported a different myth—namely, that teenagers expect their own mothers to assume responsibility for their children. Our research suggests instead that young mothers may regard the responsibility of caring for a child as a path to maturity, even choosing to leave home in order to raise their child more independently. Others, who come from disrupted homes, may experience motherhood as an incentive for "moral reform," leading them to change their lives in order to provide their children with a more stable home life than they had themselves.

Teen motherhood, and especially single motherhood, is also viewed as a problem because it is assumed that pregnancy and motherhood causes girls to drop out of school, spoiling their future job prospects and hence their ability to support a child without government aid. For some teenagers, dropping out of school in fact precedes their pregnancy and decision to have a child. For them, motherhood and the desire to provide a good future for their child sometimes produces new motivation for returning to school, particularly once their child has reached school age. But, for girls in school, it does indeed seem difficult to combine pregnancy and early motherhood with school work. Some girls are embarrassed to attend school while they are pregnant, and most schools provide little support and make few allowances for mothers. Lack of affordable and reliable day care, transportation costs, and inflexible school schedules and age specifications are among the many difficulties that teen mothers face when they try to go back to school after their child is born.

Under the current circumstances, then, the assumption that teen motherhood will disrupt schooling is not a myth. But it may be worth questioning the assumption that young women should complete their education before starting a family, since this expectation is delaying motherhood for many women well past their twenties, not to mention promoting abortion as a solution to pregnancy among college-going women. Social policies that support young women's desire for both an education *and* a family, and a greater range of choices for combining the two, are thus worth considering. An example of such a progressive policy is provided by schools that have developed special programs, including on-site day care, to help teen mothers return to and stay in school.

Finally, another common assumption is that teen mothers have chosen to have babies in order to get access to welfare benefits. As we have said before, most pregnancies are not deliberately planned, but accidental. Studies suggest that welfare may nonetheless be an important source of income for young mothers. While they might see welfare as a temporary option, however, few plan to spend their lives on it. Like older mothers, they find that it is hard to live on meagre welfare allowances, even to cover basic necessities. But given the unreliability of low-paid jobs, along with the additional costs of child care, the teen mothers we interviewed often concluded that staying on welfare was the more responsible course of action while their child was of pre-school age.

In this book, teenagers speak for themselves about getting pregnant and their experiences in opting for abortion, for adoption or to keep their baby. We hear about their considerations, how a decision took shape in the particular context of their lives, and how their decisions have worked out. Their experiences show us that, even though the options available to a pregnant teenager may be limited, the ways these options play out in individual lives vary enormously. And, as we have discovered in our own research, these "insider" accounts almost always qualify the negative assumptions and stereotypes that "outsiders" have about teen pregnancy and teen mothers, by showing us the context in which their decisions were made.

Margaret McKinnon, University of Ottawa
Prue Rains, McGill University, Montreal
Linda Davies, McGill University, Montreal

tells her

I was fifteen when I gave the baby up. I had been seeing Tom for a year, my first boyfriend. I started dating him in Grade 9, when I was fourteen. I went out with Tom for about a year before I felt ready to even have sex. I was a virgin when I met him, and the very first time we had sex, I got pregnant. I wasn't using birth control. I don't know why I didn't use anything. I was pressured into it by my boyfriend. I certainly consented, it wasn't forced upon me when we had sex that time, but I didn't feel ready. It was just in the heat of the moment and I loved him so much, I wanted to do it. It was his first time as well.

Eve and I went to three different restaurants before we found somewhere that she felt was "just right" to tell her story of being pregnant at fifteen and deciding to place her child for adoption.

I was in Grade 8 when I first saw him. He was an altar boy at church. I didn't know who he was, but I thought he was so attractive. Then, at a school dance, he asked me to dance. He asked me to go to a movie and there was the awkward thing. He wrote me a letter saying, "I had my eye on you as soon as you came to the school. I never thought you'd be interested in going out with me." And all these compliments: "You're perfect. You're my dream girl." We wrote tons of letters back and forth. After school we would go out for coffee and french fries, and smoke and talk.

Tom and I were very much in love, we wanted to be married someday. We wrote these things to each other. For our month anniversary, he'd send me flowers, buy me things, little jewellery things. We were always holding hands, cuddling. Then it progressed. I told my mom that I met this guy and that I really liked him. She was happy, she felt I was ready to go out with boys. My mother was pretty smart, pretty together. We had a super great relationship. My mom's a teacher in the Catholic school.

My mom is divorced. I have a younger brother. My mom and dad split up when I was really young, about five. He was irresponsible and she was unhappy. I didn't really know him. I haven't gone out of my way to know him, I don't really care to. I do and I don't. I don't really know the man, so I don't really feel a lot. There are many strong women in my family, but I feel the loss of not having a male influence in my life. My dad was an alcoholic, so my mom had to separate herself from the Church a little bit. She said you have to take what you can out of the religion and live by it, but she certainly didn't believe in a lot of the bullshit. She was always a feminist. She felt that just because a woman doesn't have a penis is no reason why she shouldn't be a priest. She had a lot of problems with the Church. She knew she got a messed-up upbringing in terms of sex, and she always told me that sex isn't bad, that we're human and it's a good thing. You just have to make sure you're ready.

I went to a Catholic high school. It's kind of making excuses for myself, but they basically said abstain. They didn't say if you do have sex, use a condom, nothing like that. It was just, "Don't do it. You shouldn't be doing it. You're too young. It's a sin." Getting a sexually transmitted disease wasn't even an issue. No one ever brought that up at school with my peers or with teachers. I knew STDs existed, through friends talking, other people having them. But it was never a reality in our little circle.

None of my friends had had sex yet except my best friend, who had had sex three weeks before I did. We were the first in our group that were really doing it. Tom and I had fooled around a lot, from smooching to feeling, but quite slowly. That lasted a year. He really wanted to have sex. We talked about it for three months before we actually did it. I just kept saying, "I'm not ready." During that time I was very afraid of it, the idea of doing it, the act. I didn't know what it was going to be like. It was such a big thing, such an adult thing. There was the fear of being pregnant, but not really knowing how it worked.

That day I was with a friend and we popped in to say hi, 'cause Tom only lived about two blocks from me. His parents weren't home. My friend left and we started smooching and hugging and then he said, "Do you want to?" I said, "Sure, why not?" We had had oral sex, a lot of fondling. A lot of it was me wanting more, wanting to experience the feeling. I was still afraid, but I had the feeling I could have changed my mind at any time. I knew he would not be angry or freak out in any way if I said no. There was pressure in him asking all the time, but it was very gentle. I was pretty assertive with him. I called the shots more than he did in the relationship. He knew he couldn't push it too far with me. But I loved him and he wanted something that I did want to give him. I wanted to please him.

I felt untouchable. I certainly didn't know that he should have pulled out. I thought there were only a few days in my monthly cycle when I could get pregnant, chances are it's not going to be tonight. I thought, you can't get pregnant that easily. He was nervous and excited. He said, "I think it's perfect. I love you. I want you to be my first." I said, "I would love to too, but I just don't know if I feel comfortable with it right now." I didn't make a conscious decision in my head, that I was finally ready. It was terrible. He didn't know what the hell he was doing and I didn't know. It wasn't pleasurable. He was very clumsy and I certainly didn't orgasm. He did.

We didn't actually have sex again till I found out I was pregnant. Then we had sex one more time. Once I found out I was pregnant, I didn't really want to have sex, but I felt safe doing it. I was baby-sitting and I actually enjoyed it physically. We wrote letters about how wonderful it was doing this big thing. He said how great it was. I didn't lie and say it was great. But it was really too big to talk about. I didn't tell my mom. I knew she would have thought it was too early, that I was too young. She had been asking all the time, "Are you and Tom having sex? Do you want to do anything?" I just said no, because I didn't want my mother to know that I even thought about sex.

I told Tom right away that first month when my period didn't come. But I said I wasn't going to worry about it yet. We were both lying to ourselves, but we were both nervous too. I thought, maybe I'll get so stressed out that I'll make myself not get my period. For the next four months, I was completely living in denial about what happened. My best friend had just had her first sexual experience and didn't get her period for three months after, so I thought maybe the first time you have sex it screws up your ovaries and your body is just adjusting. I thought, "I'm not going to panic, I'll just wait. Maybe it's my head, I'm just nervous." So I waited until four months, when my mother came to me and said, "Eve, I notice you haven't been using the pads and tampons, is there a chance that you could be pregnant?" I said, "No, of course not." It was just a big fear. That was the last thing I wanted my mother to know. I thought she'd be disappointed, she'd be appalled, she'd be furious. So I just denied it. She said, "Why don't we go to the doctor to make sure, just in case?" I agreed to do that.

There are things called novenas in the Catholic faith. It's like a prayer you say every day. So I was doing a novena every day in the hopes that, if I prayed enough, I wouldn't be pregnant. I was thinking that, although I sinned by having sex before marriage, I didn't use birth control, and since it's a sin to use birth control, maybe God will let me off. Really bargaining with God, hoping that I would not be pregnant.

We went to visit the doctor, and sure enough, I had a pregnancy test and it was positive. My mother was a basket case afterward. She was bawling. There was no room for me to even be upset. I was like, "Why are you crying? This is happening to me." I felt it was a role reversal, in a way. It was her caring for me, her love for me, but she was such a mess in that doctor's office that I felt I had to be the strong one. From that point, we went home and she was wonderful, much better than I would have ever thought. I was petrified. I was four months pregnant and I had already noticed a bit of discharge from my breasts.

The day I found out I was pregnant, I went back to school in the afternoon. I told Tom in the back lane and he burst out crying. He was a sobbing mess. I may have shed a few tears, but I was never wrecked. I just don't break down in front of people.

My mom was wonderful. She sat me down and she said, "We can do anything. You can have an abortion. You can give it up for adoption. But I'm not willing to help you raise a child. That's out of the question. If you want to raise the child, that's fine, but I will not raise the child for you, I already raised my kids." She wanted me to have all my options open, but she didn't think that raising a child was a realistic option. I immediately didn't think that was a realistic option either. I have always been ambitious and wanted to do things, and I thought there's no way that I want to do that with the rest of my life. Anyway, I didn't think I'd do it very well. Also, my boyfriend had cheated on me and he was kind of a creep. I certainly didn't want to make a child with him.

My mother did lean toward the adoption idea. She opened the abortion idea and said she'd have no problem with it. I was petrified of abortion. I was pro-life because of my schooling and my upbringing. At high school, we were taught pro-life. I was too naïve to question anything. Abortion sounded like the easiest way, but I was really scared of killing a baby, the moral idea of that. We didn't seriously look into it.

A few people in my family knew: my grandmother and an aunt and uncle. They all understood and were wonderful. I never got any strange feedback from them, except from my grandmother, who said, "Be sure you don't tell anyone, because they'll think you're dirty or lewd." I thought, Jesus

Christ! 'cause I really knew I wasn't.

Strange things happened, too. When I found out I was pregnant, someone actually mailed my mother a letter anonymously, about me and what a slut I was. I was really a "Goody Two Shoes" when I was in high school. I was very concerned about what the teachers thought of me. I was a teacher's pet, I got good grades, I was a cheerleader. I certainly wasn't a slut. It had been my first time. It was very disturbing. My mom had to tell me that she got this letter. She was wonderful, she knew it was ridiculous, but she wanted to tell me. She was trying to figure out why people were so concerned about my life and what was going on.

My mother told Tom's parents, with my blessing. I felt it was appropriate that he had to deal with it with his parents. His parents were looking down on me, that it was my fault, I must have enticed him into having sex. They were going to offer money or whatever to make it better. They weren't very supportive in the long run. They weren't very understanding or very generous. My mom was angry at Tom and at his parents for not being supportive. His parents wanted us to get married and have the baby. Tom would have accepted that, but I didn't want it. Tom wanted to be with me the rest of his life.

I was fifteen, in Grade 10. I didn't want anyone to know. It was clearly of huge importance to me, the purity of the young girl. I had to be popular, heaven forbid people didn't like me. I had to be a polite and good girl. I'm sure that came from my mother a little bit and from the Catholic Church and the school's influence. If someone's pregnant in that school, they were immediately out of the group, out of the fun, the dances, the boys, the social activities. The guidance counsellor and the principal would talk to girls upon finding out that they were pregnant, and encourage them to go and study privately at this place that was run by the nuns. The school wanted to keep a crystal clean image. As a Catholic high school, they didn't want a bunch of young girls going to school pregnant. So they would hide these girls at this place. I didn't want my friends to know or anyone in my family. I didn't want to be thought of as a slut. That was the biggest thing: "What are people going to think of me? My life is over. People will think I'm a slut, easy, no good, a tramp, a whore."

My mom came up with a plan. It was June, school was almost up. My mom suggested that I visit my aunt and uncle who I'm very close to and love dearly, who live in Vermont. She said, "You could go spend the summer with them if you don't want anyone to find out. No one has to know. You can stay a little longer depending on when you deliver, September or October, and you can make up whatever story you want. You are just going to Vermont to hang out with your aunt and uncle." I don't think she was pushing it, but she knew how important it was for me. I probably cried more to her about people finding out than anything else. The social thing was my greatest fear in the world, not thinking about nine months down the road or what labour was going to be like.

I was interested in dance. I decided to tell everyone at school that I was going to ballet school there. The last month of school, I hid it. I wore a lot of panty girdles to keep my stomach in, baggy clothes. Luckily, it didn't show very much at four months, but I was getting a bit of a pot.

Before I went away, Tom cheated on me a few times. The first time was with this girl we hung around with. She flirts with a lot of guys. She did very strange things. She said to me one day before I was pregnant, "Me and Tom have fooled around." But I trusted Tom implicitly, so I said, "You're so screwed up, I don't believe you at all. You can't break us up." One day, she was phoning me and pestering, so I said, "OK, the three of us are going to sit down and thrash this out, 'cause I can't stand it any more." But he said, "Forget it." That's when I thought, my god, maybe this is true. So he had cheated on me. I don't think they slept together, but they fooled around. That was big. We broke up. I didn't want to see him any more. During that week when we broke up, he smooched with another girl. I was so stressed about it. The idea that he would cheat on me when I was going through such stress was unbelievable. We had this argument, but I felt I needed him, I needed his support. I was about to go away and I loved him. I said I was disgusted, but I knew there was nothing I could do. He would admit to me that he had these feelings for other people, but I knew he wanted to be with me more than anyone else.

When we went to the airport, it was very sad. My mom came and Tom on his motorcycle with his helmet. I was very sad to leave him and go through this thing all alone, with these family members that I did love but didn't know that intimately. So I was quite devastated about that and he was devastated. He was very shaken up and petrified. I was sobbing as I was going through the boarding gate. I knew as I was leaving that me and Tom were finished. It felt terrible. We were talking about resuming the relationship when I returned; something intuitively told me otherwise.

The flight to Vermont was terrible. I was very sick on the plane. I took Gravol to settle my stomach, but it only made me sicker. Emotionally, I was a basket case, because I had to leave my boyfriend that I loved like crazy.

When I was away, I wanted to believe that it wasn't over. When I first got there, I got a few letters weekly. Then they slowed down, and that's when I had to start telling myself the truth. It had been a month and I hadn't received anything, not a phone call, not a letter. I started thinking about whether I really wanted to return to that relationship, knowing that he had cheated on me those times, knowing that he wasn't being very supportive. I started writing this poem that I worked on for about three months, which was my dealing with the fact that it was over, and it was my goodbye letter to him. I loved him. I wanted to be loved. That's what my poem was all about. "I loved you well, I loved you faithfully, and you ruined it. It's your fault." I blamed him completely.

I took a few correspondence courses in Vermont. I stayed home a lot, studying. I was watching soap operas. There was very little for me to do. Most of my friends didn't really write to me. I had confided in my best friend before I went away. She did not tell one soul, which must have been difficult for her. I was really disappointed, because I wrote her several letters. I wrote them on toilet paper and said, "Read this and then destroy it." I was so worried that people would find out. I really needed someone to correspond with me. But she only wrote me a couple of letters, not enough. I received one phone call from Tom. I only spoke to my mother while I was in Vermont.

My aunt was very supportive, she was wonderful. She's a

beautiful woman, very smart, very open. She's a social worker herself. Any questions I had, I could ask her. She was like a mother to me. I could do anything I wanted. I felt at home there, as much as I could in somebody else's home. I didn't feel any pressure in terms of cleaning. I knew I could lie on the couch and watch TV all day and do nothing, while my aunt and uncle were at work. They were both very generous, too. There were no financial worries. My mom sent them a bit of money to help.

But it was a hard time, living in a different city with no friends or family around that I really knew. I was taking all these walks, but it was a small community. I had these wicked cravings for white chocolate all the time, so I'd walk down to the grocery store. I was always hungry. I had to quit smoking. I had to eat well. I had to take iron pills. I wanted to be with my friends, hanging out at the store, smoking cigarettes, going for coffee, eating french fries. I was crying quite frequently. I was crying because of loneliness, of being in a strange place, fear of the next five months, the delivery.

I knew the basics, biologically, about the process of giving birth. I was afraid of the pain and the emotions, what was going to come up. I was thinking, oh my god, I hope I don't feel like I'm making the wrong decision once I see him or her. I didn't mention that to anybody. I always feel that I have to be strong and not lay any burdens on anybody else. So every couple of evenings, I'd have my cry and listen to a lot of Whitney Houston.

My aunt took me to my doctor appointments once a month, to see how much weight I was gaining, if I had enough iron. She went with me to the prenatal classes. That was strange: it was all couples, and I'm there with my aunt and I'm fifteen and I certainly looked very young. I don't think I ever felt embarrassed, but I felt out of place. I didn't feel that I should have been there; I felt I had made a mistake, it shouldn't have been happening to me. I felt I am too young to be going through it, I shouldn't have gotten pregnant in the first place. In my head I was hearing, "If you're mature and old enough to have sex, you're mature and old enough to use birth control."

When I got closer to the date, my mother flew down to be with me for the delivery. She just took a chance, hoping that it would happen. Luckily, the day she got there, that night my water broke and I went to the hospital. My labour went through the whole night. I got an epidural. It was a fairly easy delivery. It's hard to remember, it went pretty fast. I had a baby boy on October 14.

It was a very emotional time. A huge thing that struck me was being pregnant for nine months. Of course I knew, being pregnant, that there was a baby in my stomach. But the huge revelation when I actually gave birth to the baby and saw him—it was so powerful to realize that the baby came out of me. It was the most intense thing in my life. I was very happy about my situation, thrilled because I saw him. I created a life. That was wonderful. I certainly don't want to sound like a pro-lifer, because I'm not at all right now. I can still say I'm proud of my decision. Whether I would do the same thing again, I don't know. But it is a powerful experience to see a life. I'm really happy that I did give a life to a family that couldn't have a baby, that there's a little bit of joy in that family. Also that I'm physically capable of having a baby, biologically, just to know that I can do it. Quite an intense experience.

I had originally thought that, when I had the baby, I wouldn't even look at it. I made the decision that, if I didn't look at it, it would be easier. But I spoke to a doctor who I thought was quite bright. He said, "You're free to do that, I understand where you're coming from. But you might not deal with it emotionally, you might not allow yourself the reality that you did have a baby unless you look at him, and then you can work it out." I thought about that a lot, and I thought it was important for me to see him. So I did see him immediately after the delivery, as well as the next day and the next day. I bottle-fed him and held him a little bit over the next couple of days, just to admit to myself that I had him, to see what he looked like, to take a few pictures, to have a concrete memory. And I'm glad I did that.

I had seen the social worker about the adoption a few times before the delivery. She asked me a lot of questions. She counselled me about my relationship, why I hadn't used birth control. She filled me in on different methods of birth control. She was a very warm and loving woman. She asked me what kind of family I'd like to see the baby go to. I was shocked. She asked if I wanted them to be a religious family, any special qualities that I wanted them to have. I said the religion didn't matter, but I wanted the mother to be quite strong and independent and definitely in an equal partnership. That was the only specific thing I gave her. She said I could write a letter to the baby. I could give the adoptive parents something to give to him when he gets to be a certain age, based on their discretion. She didn't guarantee that the adoptive parents would give it to him, but she said she would pass along anything I wanted. I collected poetry in a journal, so at the back of that journal I wrote a letter to him, assuming he was at a rational age, like a teenager, when he could understand everything. I tried to explain why I was doing it, why I gave him up for adoption, so he would know it wasn't a desertion, it was not that I didn't want him. I explained my feelings for his father and why I couldn't keep him.

After having the baby and knowing that I was giving it up, I didn't ever want to go back on my decision. I didn't want to take the baby home. I still knew, rationally, that I was not ready. I did not want to raise that baby, both for him and for me. But at the same time, it was a terrible feeling, just leaving him at the hospital. That was very strange. One of the strangest moments was leaving the hospital. I was leaving with all my plants and flowers that everyone had sent me, and I was in the elevator with another woman. I was in the wheelchair, 'cause they don't want you to fall over or anything, and she had all her plants and flowers and a baby and I just had the plants and flowers in my arms. I was feeling, "Something is clearly missing here. I'm forgetting something." That was really strong. I'll never forget that—that elevator, being paired up with a woman taking her baby home.

They gave me pills to dry up the breast milk. I was sore with stitches and whatever, but I healed incredibly fast. My stomach flattened right away. Normally it takes time for your stomach to go back down after. Usually you look pregnant for a good couple of weeks after you have the baby.

When I got back, I had a lot of school work to catch up on. I had missed two months. Because my aunt and uncle ate so healthily, I probably looked better than when I left. My friends knew something was up. People probably noticed my belly before I left, but when I got back I was thinner. So the rumour going around school was that I had gone to the States and had an abortion. I just denied it to everybody who asked me. It was clear I didn't want to talk about it, and when I did, I told them all this bullshit. They wouldn't let it die. They said, "You're lying to me. Why are you lying to me?" And I thought to myself, "Maybe this is a lie I'm telling you. Can't you just accept it?" But I stuck to my guns and pretended there was this whole other story. They wouldn't accept that as the truth. There were a lot of bad experiences like that. People were coming down really hard on me, wanting to know the truth. I felt very different about my friends, mainly because they let me down in terms of support, even if they kept my story.

Tom had confided in a couple of people, and I was really resentful of that. I got no money from him, he didn't have to go through anything, all he had to do was live his life as normal, and he couldn't even keep his mouth shut. Him talking about it was really shitty. I knew there were people that he had to talk to, but there are people you can trust and those you can't. He told it to the big drinkers, the party goofs, the assholes. He told a teacher in school at a private meeting. Then I realized that that teacher went on to tell every other teacher. But since I came back three months late, I had to confide in a few of the teachers and tell them what happened anyway, in order to get back into school. Eventually it faded away and people didn't give a shit any more. It took around the whole year for people to finally let it go. I thought it would go much smoother than it did, and I thought it would die off much faster than it did. When I look at the yearbook for the following year, people wrote in it, "All bad things pass by," "Hope you're doing well"—insinuating stuff. One person signs your book like that and other people read it. I thought, holy shit, everyone thinks I'm a mess.

Me and Tom, that was a whole other story. My cousin, who's two years younger than me, came to visit every summer. She knew Tom, and the three of us really got along well. Well, the summer I was having the baby, they got together. I found out about this when I was in Vermont, because she got caught staying out all night. That was the final, that was the very big one. I was like, "Uh, uh, no more. That's my blood and my family, and that's terrible. Be with whoever you want, but come on, my cousin?" He was waiting for me at the airport when I got back, and he had flowers and the whole bit. I was polite, but I said, "I don't want to see you ever again. Just keep your mouth shut." I wrote some stupid poems and gave them to him.

The next couple of years were fine. I let it go. I thought about the baby. The people who adopted him sent me a picture when he was six months old, which I really appreciated. When they're first born, they put this little cut-off sock or toque on their heads, 'cause they lose heat through their heads. I kept that, as well as some pictures I took of me and of my family holding him in the hospital room. I can still smell his hand. I would really love another picture. Maybe now he looks like me. I would love to see him. I would not want to interfere at all, as I didn't want to interfere then either. I never went through a big longing for him, more a curiosity as to what he's like, what his little personality is like, what his parents are like, how he's doing.

I didn't ever imagine my life with him. I would just wish him well, send my personal little messages that I'm sure weren't received. I am curious, not really knowing if he's alive or what. In October, the month of his birthday, I always remember him. I felt good on Mother's Day. It felt like a little tribute to myself, a coy kind of knowing that I have something to celebrate on that day. It was never really difficult, but I've always been optimistic and don't retain negative thoughts. That's my nature.

Going through the delivery, as difficult as it was for me, was a huge, a really wonderful experience. If I died today—knowing I've brought a child into this world, a contribution, a sacrifice—in a sense it would be something to be proud of. I feel that I matured through the last few months of the pregnancy and the last few months of that year. I felt different from other people. I felt very good about myself. I was feeling much more cautious about my language and the words I used, thinking more before I speak, in case I'm offending someone or I'm being insensitive to someone, because I felt that so much before I went away. I became more intuitive. If someone doesn't want to share something with me, their personal space, maybe I shouldn't push it. I felt a bit more serious. I could still let go and have a good time, but I couldn't be as silly because I've got more of a conscience. I don't mean guilt, just more sensitive to others.

Up till then, sex still hadn't been that pleasurable an experience for me. It wasn't something I was missing or wanting. My next relationship lasted four months, but I didn't have sex with him—partly out of fear of pregnancy, even though at that time I was on the pill. I was not about to make the same mistake again. It just wasn't something I was ready to touch again. It was a big issue in that relationship. I was older then, and it was more the norm in a relationship. He was like, "I don't understand, why not?" I didn't tell him about the baby. The biggest thing in my head was protection.

If there was no protection, it wasn't even an option. Not the greatest heat of any moment would make me do that.

I'm definitely pro-choice now. This week I saw some pro-life supporters, men with placards. If there's anything I want to do, I want to knock those guys on their ass. It's a woman's decision. When I was in Vermont, coming from a pro-life stance in my life 'cause that's all I really knew, I saw assholes on TV preaching pro-life stuff to me. Even though I was having the baby and giving it up for adoption, seeing those men telling women what they should do, I was furious. If I were having an abortion, how much more infuriated I would be.

About the adoption, I think I made the right choice. I think if I had married Tom and kept the baby, that would have been a nightmare, not because of the baby so much, but because of our relationship. But if my mother had pushed abortion, I probably would have had an abortion. I was following the influence of people around me. I knew she preferred adoption, but an abortion wouldn't have changed our relationship. I've always known my mom has loved me unconditionally since the day I was born. I certainly knew that, if I had an abortion, she would love me, she would respect my decision, she would be behind me.

I'm proud of the fact that I had the baby, and I feel good that he's alive and living with his family. On his birthday, I always think of him and try to buy a piece of pie and sing a happy birthday song to myself to him. I'll never look for him, because I don't think it's my place, but I really hope he contacts me one day. I would love to meet him, get to know him. It's a terrible thing for a young woman to go through, for someone who isn't ready. It's a hard decision to make when you don't even know who you are yet.

Katrina

tells her

My baby's name is Daniel. His dad's name is Dan. I didn't really have choice with that. If it had been a girl, I would've been able to name a girl. Oh well, I'm happy. His dad's happy with the baby. He's a lot older than me. He's twenty-four now, I'm turning nineteen. I was sixteen, he was twenty-one when I got pregnant. Daniel will be two next month. He's cute, a very energetic, very happy little guy, so I can't complain.

Daniel's dad is Chinese. My parents are, you know, old European parents. Oh my god, I thought my father would blow up. You know, Daniel would be mixed, right? And on top of everything I was sixteen when I had him. I still hadn't finished high school.

My mother at first wanted me to have an abortion, and to get her off my back I told her I'd think about it. But she took it as "I'll do it." I ended up not doing it, so when I did tell her I didn't have it done and it was too late, she blew up totally. My father didn't know I had a baby until a month after my son was born. I lived at home, but when I was six months pregnant, I moved out to live with my boyfriend's cousin.

What happened was, I wasn't using anything and then I started on birth control. It was only the first month and I got pregnant. It was really odd because I hadn't used—it was like the withdrawal method, and we weren't too worried about it. My friend then got pregnant using withdrawal and I said to myself, whoaa! So I went to the doctor and he gave me my first pack of birth-control pills for free and told me to come back and get a prescription and get it filled all the time. I said OK, no problem. Then it was the first two, three weeks, I gather, that I must've gotten pregnant while using it. I thought it was totally weird. That's my luck.

I had missed my period, and I had got really sick when I was pregnant—like, throwing up all the time. They ended up giving me Gravol, because by the end of three months I was throwing up so heavily, I was throwing up blood. I was feeling nauseous in the morning. I usually don't. Usually I'm up early in the morning, rummaging through the fridge looking for something to eat. So I went and got that blood test and the next day they ended up calling my boyfriend's house with the results. I didn't want them calling my parents' house. He got the news first. He called me and said, "Come over, I have a surprise for you." I was thinking the doctor called and said I'm not pregnant, and I was really happy. So I go down there and I said, "So tell me, tell me, tell me." And I was expecting him to say, "You've got the stomach flu" or some wacky thing. I sat there. He said, "Well, it's good news, the test came out positive." And I said, "The test came out positive?" And he's like, "Aren't you happy?" And I'm like, well, I'm thinking, yeah, kind of. "Well, I'm happy you're happy." I was, like, in shock!

I knew he wanted to have a baby. All the comments he had made. It wasn't a forced thing where I had to have one right now, but if this opportunity came along, I knew he would take it if possible. So we talked. We talked about financially what would happen. He didn't really ask me if I wanted the baby, he just asked me what I would do. I told him what I thought, that I didn't want to have an abortion, but I was scared to have a baby seeing as I was so young. I was scared about what my parents would say. I had really mixed feelings at that point because I knew he wanted to have the baby. He said, "Don't worry, I'll get a job, you can finish school."

We talked over a few days about what our different options were. We finally figured out that either I could have an abortion, which neither of us was really going for, or we could give the baby up for adoption, but that was another one of those really way-out options, because after carrying the child for nine months I don't think that I could easily just say, "Here, take it." The other option was to live with his parents. His parents were very supportive of him, the decisions that he made. So I knew his parents weren't going to turn me away if there were problems. I felt that I had some support there. His brothers and sisters, we all get along really well. They're really nice people. There's never been a conflict with me being white.

I chose to have my baby because I was on this morality trip where abortion is bad and wrong. You should always have your children. You don't even think about it, you know, you have your children. This is the only child God might give you. Plus I said, "I wanted to have a baby. I got pregnant, and if I was old enough to lay down and have sex, then I should be old enough to take my responsibility on, right?"

I was kind of happy, but I was really, really scared. Really scared. I mean, I made all these plans and I didn't even tell my mother. I was scared of telling my mother. I was scared of telling my father. My father is a really big man and when he gets mad he gets really...he starts going on rampages, so I was really scared. My mother and me have always been closer than me and my father. But I was scared of telling her because my mother is a "dictative" person.

It was really weird because my mom and dad have never talked about abortion. It's always been, "You're just going to keep your baby if you ever get pregnant." But they were never expecting me to get pregnant so early. They were expecting me to get married, finish school and then have a baby. Not the totally opposite way. When I first got pregnant, my mom told me to have an abortion. I asked her, "Why would you want me to do something like that? You've always told me Christian this, Catholic that, you know, go to church..." She was always really into church and all that, and she was like, "When I was young I had an abortion." That was the first time I'd heard about it. She was my age. And she goes, it was one of the best decisions she's made, because she could've ruined her whole life. So I said, "OK, Mom, I'm not going to have an abortion. I'm going to keep the baby." She said, "What are you going to do?" And when I told her my plans, she said, "How can you even think of doing that? You're so young. How could you go out and have your own household? You don't even clean your own room, for God's sake." So I said, "I've done a lot of growing up." She tried to talk me into giving the baby up for adoption, but then when he was actually born, she came to see him in the hospital, she ended up bringing me diapers and baby stuff and clothes and all that stuff. As soon as she saw him she totally came around.

I think she was more worried about my difficulty with my father, that his grandchild is half Chinese. My father is a prejudiced person. He's racist. I don't even want to go into him, he's like friggin' Hitler. And if he's not making a nasty comment about another race, he's making a nasty comment about my mother.

Me and my father didn't have a very good relationship. We did when I was very young. Up to the age where I would say, "Yes, Daddy, whatever you say, Daddy," and then do what he says, everything was fine. Once I hit the time where I would say, I want to go hang out with my friends or I want this kind of hairstyle instead of the one you want me to wear, I want to wear these kinds of clothes, not what you want me to wear, I want to listen to this type of music, not your type of music, we started getting into altercations. Big time. It happened over a period of time. If he would get mad, I would get mad, then he would yell, and I would start yelling, and then he'd start hitting and I would yell even worse.

We went through the family court system. My father was put on an order that he was not to use any corporal punishment on any of his children. Now that I live here, away from him, and I go over there, if he makes a comment that I don't like, I just keep my mouth shut. If he keeps going on, I just leave. And now we have a lot better relationship. He can't really do anything to me now. I live here. I don't feel as trapped as I did when I lived there. It was wicked.

There was a really good counsellor at my old high school. A lot of students liked her because she helped a lot. She would go out of her way to come and get you if you were in trouble. She was your friend. She was amazing. I went to school until I was seven months pregnant, then I did Home Instruction. I saw her until I left. She helped me out a lot because she presented me with the choices that I had. She told me it was OK to choose to do what I wanted to do, but I already knew, deep down in my heart, that I was going to keep the baby.

So I ended up having Daniel. It was a twelve-hour labour. I went into labour at two o'clock in the morning. I started getting really strong cramps. I waited until four in the morning before getting my friend and telling her to go and call the hospital and to call my boyfriend. Because I thought, what if it's false labour, 'cause it was two weeks early. So they took me to the hospital. That's when my mom came to visit me. My boyfriend was there the whole time before I had the baby. He saw everything. He said it looked like a watermelon coming out. Hey, a little humour, he likes to joke around a lot. His whole family came to visit me that day. Except his parents. I don't know, I think they were working or something.

I've been pregnant three times. First time was with Daniel, the second time I had an abortion. The second pregnancy was when I didn't know what was going on with my life. I was so totally confused. I went to a party with my friends. So we were drinking that night and over the period of a few days, I forgot to take my pill, and I don't even know what I was doing. I was purposely destroying myself. I knew that if you missed a few days or even one day, you're at risk to get pregnant. I knew this and I still had sex with my boyfriend with no condom, nothing, and it was because of my own neglect.

Daniel was not even a year yet. I think it was just so hard with everything. I knew that I was hurting myself, but it was like, who cares? I didn't really care. I don't know what actually made me do that, now I realize how stupid it was.

I told Dan. I mean, I'm not going to hide it from him. We had already discussed it. If I was to get pregnant again, we knew that there was no way we could keep another baby. No way possible, I was still in high school. I still couldn't believe it. I just thought, this can't be happening to me.

I was nine weeks pregnant when I had the abortion. When I actually went into the abortion, it was like a relief. I wasn't nervous. I wasn't upset. I was actually thinking, once I get this over with, no one's going to know. And it's going to be over, it's going to be done with, I'm going to be able to go home and pretend like nothing ever happened. I was not nervous. I was so cold-hearted, it wasn't funny. When I think back on it now, I just don't understand how I could even be like that.

The second abortion, I was bawling my eyes out the night before. The first time, I just wanted to get it over with. The second time, though, when I got pregnant I couldn't have another baby. There wasn't even an option. I didn't want to have another baby because it was really hard with the first one, with Daniel—financially, school work, my mother. There's no way I could take care of another baby. My life would be ruined if I had that baby.

Now I'm crying. It's this second abortion. I keep thinking

about it. It's really hurting me. It'll be OK. I just need some time. I just got it over with. It's, like, a week yesterday. It was something I had to do. This time, what happened is, I was taking the birth-control pill. I got tonsillitis. So they gave me antibiotics, but they didn't tell me the antibiotics would interfere with the pill. I had no clue that antibiotics would interfere with the pill. So when I got pregnant, it was like, this can't be happening again. How does this happen? I was religious about the pill. This time I felt like a slut. It wasn't that I was sleeping with a whole bunch of men; I felt like I was using abortion as a method of birth control. How could I do this a second time?

Both the times, Dan would say to me, "Isn't there any way we can keep the baby?" No. It does not work financially, 'cause I'm already strained with all the bills: Daniel, diapers, food, everything that comes down. Not only would we be financially strained, but there's no way I could handle it emotionally, mentally. I've got so much school work to do. Last year I went to summer school to keep my son in day care. It's a subsidized day care, but you have to be in school or work four hours a day to qualify for the program. So I'm looking for a full-time job. It's hard to get nowadays. If I can't get that, I'm going to be taking summer school courses.

The second abortion was a lot harder. I can't cry in front of my boyfriend. It's not that I can't, but I don't want to. I don't want to show him that it's affecting me the way that it is. I don't know. It's just so...so personal. Maybe he wouldn't understand. He says to me sometimes, "Crying is a sign of weakness." I'm like, "No it's not. It's part of strength. That you have strength to be able to cry in front of somebody else and still feel decent about yourself." I just don't want him to know how much it hurts me, because then he'll say, "Then why didn't you have the baby?" It's just that I know it's going to be a no-win situation with him if I tell him. He just won't understand where I'm coming from. With him, there would always be some kind of answer. So I'll just leave it. I'm OK.

I'll get over it. And I'm promising myself never to go through it again. Never again in my life. 'Cause this time hurt too much. Now, no matter what happens, if I feel I'm at any risk of getting pregnant, there's no way anyone can force me. No one. I couldn't go through it again. I know I had to do it, but it affected me a lot more than last time. A lot different. I don't know how it could be so different. I'm comparing to the last time so much because I didn't feel like my morality was going down in any way. I feel like I let it happen. Basically, I feel like less of a person because the first time, it was only once.

My mom doesn't know about the first abortion or the second one. I know she'd be happy in a way, that I had an abortion, if I were to tell her, but she'd be really really mad at me for getting pregnant in the first place. She wouldn't even understand how I could do it. She couldn't even understand how it could happen. She'd say, "Didn't you know? Why didn't you ask?" To her it would be really simple: "How could you let it happen? Good that you did what you did, but..." I look at my mother differently now. Because I think, how could you be so Catholic and so Christian when I know you've had an abortion and you wanted me to have one? To me, I'm a non-practising Catholic. I believe in God and all that, but I don't believe in all these rules they have set out for you. If you're going to get punished, you're going to get punished by Him in the afterlife; you don't have to be punished by people here and now who aren't God and aren't perfect. If you're doing something wrong, He'll punish you, He'll take care of it after. I don't see the point in telling some priest that you did something wrong, God knows that you did something wrong. He knows if you're remorseful, if you repent your sins. So I don't know how she could be so Catholic about everything and then still hold these views about abortion—that I should have an abortion if I was pregnant. I don't understand it, but my mother's my mother. I can't change it.

I just don't want everyone to know that I did this. I wouldn't mind going and talking to somebody; I just don't want everyone to know I actually did it. It's private. It's a private thing.

I've grown up a lot since I had the first abortion, because I realize now that everything isn't so simple. You can't just say, "You can only have an abortion under the circumstances that you get raped." You have to be in the shoes of the person who's pregnant before you can tell them not to have an abortion. Sometimes I remember the protesters outside the clinic who were telling me, "Abortion hurts everybody." And I was like, "If I have this child, are you going to be there to feed it? Are you going to be there to bathe it? Are you going to be there to clothe it? Are you going to be there to watch the baby while I have to do my homework? You're telling me to keep the baby, but are you going to *be there*?! My life would be ruined if I have this baby. And no one can tell me abortion is wrong, now that I'm in this situation." It changed me totally. Now I'm a lot more open-minded than I used to be.

Me and my mom, our relationship has gotten better, and I don't want to make it worse. I'm listening to her just because of her help, all the help that she gives me with Daniel.

Watching him if I have to go to the library or if I have to do something, she's there for me.

Now, I'm not being irresponsible. I've got too much to look forward to. I'm doing really well in school. I'm finishing my first year of community college in a month and I'm so happy that I'm doing really well. I want another child, later on in life. I want to finish school, get a good job, and then when I have my wedding, I want to do it right. I want to have the flower girl, the whole bit. I want to go on a two-week honeymoon. I want to have a nice big wedding, but not yet. Maybe seven years down the road. Then that would be it, that would be my whole family.

Daniel, the love of my life, is growing and running around here. He's a little brat now and then, but it's my fault because I spoil him. Everything is going so well in my life now, and I don't want to screw it up again.

The forms at the clinic said that teens can read this book and see what they have to choose from, different options. I just wanted to call and talk to somebody, so that if somebody else is in this position, they would know that they could do this or this. They could read about it and they could say, "This is good for me, and this isn't good for me." I just went with my decisions by how I thought my life would've turned out later on.

So at least if someone's reading the book, they can see their different options. There's so much literature out there on anti-abortion/pro-life. So if there's someone out there who needs to know what's available to them...I know I'll never write a book. It's good that someone's going to.

Rose tells her story

I'm seventeen, and I got pregnant four months ago. I covered it up with clothes because I was still in school. Wait—I got mixed up. The first time was a year ago. I had an abortion. That was hard. It's really strange to find out a year later that you're in the same situation again, and I have no idea what to do. It's causing a lot of problems.

The first time I got pregnant, I had only been on birth-control a couple of months. It was really confusing because I thought nothing was supposed to happen when you were on the pill. The doctor said the pills weren't really working for me. We tried six or seven different kinds and none of them were really doing what they were supposed to.

Usually, when I go to the doctor, I do all these tests for everything and they always came back negative, so I never thought anything of it. Then the doctor called and the message was on the answering-machine. He said I was pregnant. I thought maybe he was joking or something.

Never looking me in the eye or raising her voice above a whisper, Rose sat on the edge of her bed and discussed her feelings about an abortion, having an abusive boyfriend, and being four months pregnant.

I was living in a foster home at

the time. I just didn't know what to do. For a brief second I was happy, because I love kids and I've always wanted to have a lot of kids. It's just that the timing and everything was really bad, and I wasn't sure what my real mom was going to say and what my boyfriend was going to say, because we hadn't known each other for so long.

I didn't know what to do, because before that I always had thoughts of killing myself if things didn't go right. That's what kept going through my mind, off and on. I can't do that, I have to work out my problems. It was strange. I went crazy for a week: I was crying, I was confused and I wouldn't talk to anyone. I was yelling at everyone.

My foster mom was pretty supportive. She tried to help me. She told me it was up to me. I just thought that abortion was my only way out. That way, nobody knew. It was just an easy way out of everything. I've always said to myself, I wouldn't do that, have an abortion. But I found myself doing it anyway.

I was in school, Grade 11. We were sixteen. Anthony said it wasn't the right time. I guess you could say he kind of convinced me to do what he wanted, have an abortion. I didn't want to be a problem. Anthony said that's what we should do, because we don't have the money to take care of a baby. We didn't have anywhere to go because I was in a foster home, he was living with his parents. He didn't want to tell his parents. We didn't have any support.

I knew I could've probably had the baby, if I had the money. I would've been able to take care of a child, and if not, maybe put it up for adoption. I was willing to try to keep it until I couldn't. But I usually do what other people say. With certain things I don't have a mind of my own. Ever since I was little, if someone tells me it's not right, then I just say, "OK."

When I told Anthony—the first time—when I had the abortion, I said, "It would never happen again. Even if it's three months down the road, we won't go through an abortion again, we'll have it." A year later I came to him again and said this is what's going on, and his first reaction was, let's have an abortion. It just shocked me...and he was going to break up with me because I wanted to have the baby. So now he says, let's put it up for adoption, but I can't do that either. When Anthony figures that out, he's going to leave. I couldn't give my baby up for adoption. You never know who's taking care of them, if they've killed them or not.

My foster mother and my friends said that two out of three people who have abortions the first time feel an empty void. For the past year, whenever I saw someone with a baby, I would just—I wanted it. And now I could have one. I'm getting a second chance for something that I did wrong. This time it didn't bother me at all. I knew I wanted it.

I'm religious. I'm not *really* religious, I'm not the church-going type. When I had the abortion, I felt like I was committing murder. That's what I thought. For about two months after, I just kept hearing this child crying in my head. This time, I feel like I got a second chance. I'm going to try and do it right this time. I'm going to take care of the baby myself and if I realize that I really and truly cannot do it, then I will give it to people who do need kids and who have been looking for kids. I just feel I have to try. I have to give myself that...I have to try and get rid of the pain, even though I know it won't go away.

My friends kept telling me I have to tell my mom because

I'm going to need help. Anthony doesn't know my mom knows, but I felt that I should tell her. If I decide to keep the baby, you can't come nine months later with this little newborn in your hand, it makes parents feel really heartbroken and useless. They don't feel like they can help if their child is leading a completely different life and don't want their parents involved in it.

I didn't know how my mother would react, because ever since I was little she said to me that if I ever came to her with that she would kill me. But when I told her, she never really said anything. She just said, "Oh my god, I can't believe you're making me a grandmother so early, don't you realize I'm young?" We just had a good laugh. She said, "Whatever you decide, I'll be by you." She kind of told me I can't put it up for adoption, if it comes to that just to give it to her. She said, "It's not a puppy. It's not just something you can give away because you don't want it. If you don't want it, you should've taken proper precautions to make sure you wouldn't have any in the first place."

My mom had me when she was nineteen and my grandmother took care of me. It's kind of a family tradition where I come from, for the grandmother to take care of the grandchild. As far as I was concerned, my grandmother was my mother. My mother left me for eight years. She said she tried to get me out of Cuba, to bring me here, but still that was eight years of my life that I never knew her at all.

My dad passed away when I was six. My mom remarried. My stepfather was a sick, perverted man. I never liked him at all. I remember when I first met him, he hugged me and my whole body just shook. I didn't like him. He was just—he didn't seem friendly at all. He didn't even like children. They had a child together, but he never wanted my brother. He told my mom to have an abortion. I know for a fact he didn't want children.

I guess it started when I was fourteen. I used to come home from school and he would hit me for no reason. He would call me names. He would touch me when I was asleep. He used to come in the shower with me. I told my mother. She spoke with him, but he made it look like I was lying because I just didn't want them to be together and because I just wanted to go back home. That's true, I did want to go back to my grandmother. I didn't know my mother so well and I didn't want to be with her.

I just didn't want to be there and know that, every time I went to sleep, I had to keep one eye open wondering if he was coming through the door. My mother didn't do anything about it because she believed him. For the next couple of years I didn't say anything. One day he hit me in the face with a belt and I had a scar, a weal going down my face. I went to school and everyone was saying, "What happened?" and I said, "Oh, I ran into a door." But my guidance counsellor called the police. I never really went home after that. I went to the foster home.

A month later my mom kicked my stepfather out because I said I wasn't going to come home until he was gone. I'm just glad my mom got rid of him. Then there was problems with my mom because we didn't get along, so I never went home for about two years. During all that time my life just seemed to get worse and worse. As the years go by, it's not getting any better. I always thought you go further ahead, not fall behind.

Before I got pregnant the second time, Anthony was the

most wonderful guy in the whole world. But it's like this baby has brought everything bad out of him. We've been together a year and six months. A year ago he was my ideal guy, he was my "Mr. Right." Until he started hanging out with his friends a little bit more and drinking and smoking marijuana. He became a completely different person, and that's not the type of person I want. I try to tell him that, but he just says, "I'm just doing it for fun."

Anthony doesn't want me to go outside and fall or something. I know it's not so much that I might lose the baby, he doesn't want me to be hurt in any way. He doesn't realize he's hurting me, emotionally. He's like a big child. He's very spoiled, and very complicated. He puts a lot of stress and strain on me, because I have school to worry about. I have to keep up my attendance really good or I won't graduate.

When I try to ask him something about the baby, he says, "Why do you always have to be talking about the baby?" He says I think about it too much. It's hard not to think about it when everything you do is because of your child. You have it inside of you, you can't exactly not think about it. Every morning when you go to put on your clothes and you've got this belly in front of you, you see your body changing. You can't just block it out of your mind. It's easy for him because he's not really going through it.

I still love him. We plan to be together forever and have a truckload of children. If we have a plan to be together for the rest of our lives and have all the kids in the world, what would it matter if one came now? I know I could take care of this child now. I'll be finished school by the time the baby comes, but he doesn't see it like that. He wants to...bring home the bacon. He doesn't want me to do anything else but stay home. But I can't do that. I need to feel I have some form of independence. I wouldn't mind being a housewife, but I don't want to be one forever. A year or two, fine, but the rest of my life? I don't want to be dependent on anybody, because what happens when he leaves? I'm stuck and I have to find somebody else who's going to provide for me and my kids. I want to know that I can do it myself, but he wants to do it on his own, so we're kind of apart there. And he said that, if we keep the baby, it's going to affect him. If we don't keep the baby, it's going to affect me, but still he's telling me that I cannot keep the baby. I'm just not going to be able to handle all this.

Anthony's my biggest problem right now. I have my mom, my foster mom, my sister, my friends. I have everybody that I need, but him. He takes me to the doctor's, but it doesn't mean that he really cares what's going to happen, just "Here, go have an abortion." I can't get him to even talk to me, so I can't convince him to see things my way. It is basically my decision because we're not married. I just felt he should have a say in whatever I decide because he is the father. I could've just not asked him and just done what I wanted and to hell with him.

I just won't put the baby up for adoption. It would be harder to give birth to a child knowing you're never going to take it home, you're not going to have that experience of waking up at two o'clock in the morning to feed the baby, you're not going to see it walk for the first time.

I bought a baby bottle. I'm trying not to buy a lot of things because he says, "What's the sense of buying anything when we're giving it away?" He's so set that I do that. It's like it's not my choice—my body, but not my choice. He's pretty mean. He's thrown me around a couple of times, hit me. He's very loud, yelling. I try to not get on his bad side.

I don't care if he leaves *me*, but I want my child to have a father. I didn't have one. And the one father-figure that I did have betrayed the trust that I had. I want it to have a natural father, because the biological parents are the only parents that can take care of a child better. A lot of people might disagree, but that's how I feel. My grandmother did a good job, but I know that there are things that my mother could've given me that my grandmother couldn't. It's really hard to explain, but a little baby and a mother have a bond together. It's a different kind of love. I knew my grandmother couldn't give me the kind of nurturing that a mother could give.

I have a job. I could probably get along without Anthony. My mom did it. She raised two kids by herself and she did pretty good. She says if you don't have any money, you don't have anything to give your kids. My mom didn't have anything when she came here, she made something. People can

make something out of nothing; why can't we do it? Why do we have to have everything all at once? Things don't come in a nice little package. Anthony doesn't seem to realize that. He's got these one-way-vision glasses on. He only sees what's in front of him. He won't look the other way.

I try and solve everything myself, and that causes even more problems. Because from the time I was living with my mother and my stepfather, everything that was going on I'd keep to myself, and it built up into a lot of anger and I'd get into fights at school just to try and release some anger. I went to therapy and to groups and I finally got rid of it and could talk about what was going on. Now I feel like I'm back in the same situation as my stepfather put me in, but it's somebody else. I have to keep pushing everything down. I don't want it to blow up. I don't like violence, but I thought it was the only way I could get rid of what I'm feeling.

I know that there's one thing I'll not tolerate at all, I couldn't. Anthony hasn't done it in a while, actually, but I think if I had a child right now and he was to raise his hand at my child, I think that would be the straw that broke the camel's back. I think I would kill him, because it happened to me. I don't want it happening to my kid. I don't want them to go through that pain.

I'm spending more and more time with just me and I feel I'm stuck in this corner. I feel like there's nobody there I can talk to because nobody wants to hear what I want to say. I don't want it all inside. I went through a time like that. It took two years to rebuild myself up to be somebody I can actually say I love. I don't think I have another two years to sit there in counselling again.

Everything about me is just completely changing. I was

fit. I was very athletic. I could get out there and run and do whatever I wanted. Now my body has just seemed to have lost everything. It went completely berserk. Everything about me has changed. My ankles hurt, my back hurts, I'm getting marks around my mouth. I used to have, I guess you could say, flawless skin. I considered myself to have looked good. My whole body is just changing. The fact that I can't eat what I want...I bought a nutrition book to make sure I eat properly. The book's been telling me what to eat—a lot of vegetables. I see the doctor regularly. I'm going to prenatal classes. And they're going to have a parenting class after. I'm going to take the parenting class to make sure that I do it correctly or do it the best that I know how. I have to take care. There was a time that I never slept at all. I can't do these things any more. This little defenceless child is affecting my whole life before it's even born. One good thing is, it'll keep me healthy.

To know that *my* body can make a child—I mean, I *knew* it could do that, but when you actually know it's there, when you can feel it, you have that feeling that half of your personality is in there. It's really amazing that your body could do that, your body could produce a whole human being. In just nine months. Nine months seems long, but it's a very short time for a person to be made. I'm just anxious. I want to see what the baby looks like. I want to see if it's a boy or a girl.

I would prefer a boy, because if my boyfriend does leave, a boy will be much easier on me. They don't require a lot of things, I've noticed. Even when they get older. A girl, you have to have everything. I just think it would be easier for a teenage mom who's single to have a boy. I was a tomboy, but I let guys push me around. Whenever I seemed to get close to them, I just let them do whatever they wanted. I'm going to try and make sure that doesn't happen. I know for sure I would want a boy because I've always pictured myself with a little boy. I picture him when he's one year old, the way I'm going to dress him, cut his hair. If I had a girl, it's not really going to change how I feel, but I think I want a boy. I know I do, but I think I'm going to have a girl. Whenever I want something it always comes out the opposite.

My actual plans for my life since I was little was finish school when I was seventeen and stay home for a year before I went to college. So this baby just fell right into my empty spot. It just fell right in place. It seems my life is pretty much going the way I wanted it to go. When the baby is about a year old, I was going to go to college. They have a day care there; that way you can keep an eye on the baby the whole day. For about six months after the baby's born, I will be on maternity leave. After that I will go back to work as well as be on government assistance. I would go that route until I got back on my feet and everything is organized.

Whenever I thought about that, I was hoping my boyfriend would still be with me, but if he can't then that's OK. My friend won't be in school. She said that she would take care of the baby, 'cause I won't be working all that often—maybe once or twice a week—and she'll take care of the baby while I'm gone. I won't work longer than three hours. I would pay her, but she says she doesn't want me to. I can't just let her take a six-month-old child for three hours. It's pretty dependent on everybody. If I can't do it, if I can't work as well as take care of the baby, then I guess I'll just stay home. That's what I want to do.

I have my own apartment. I pay $300 a month. The place

itself is nice, but the people, I would rather not be with. They're not really clean, and they're not really quiet. I work part-time and I'm on the "Young Adults Program" at the child protection agency. They pay my board, they give me a cheque every month. That goes for my rent, food, an allowance, and whatever else I have left. I work at KFC. That's pretty much all I do. I work and I go to school. I live a very boring life.

Maybe at first, right off the bat, I might not be the greatest mom. I might not know exactly what to do. I know how to feed a baby, but I don't know how to bath a baby and I'm afraid of that, because what if I drown it or drop it? Some things I might not know, but I'll find out. My only worry is that my kid will grow up and be something that I don't want it to be. If I do good, then chances are my kid will be good.

I want my kids to come to me and tell me *anything* no matter *what* it is or how stupid it might seem. I want them to come to me and tell me what's going on. You know? Like, "You wouldn't believe what happened to me at school." I don't want to feel like I'm the "mother," but somebody they can talk to. I want to be part of their life as much as I can. I think that's what most parents want: they want their kids to come to them, to talk.

■

I'm doing this interview because the first time I became pregnant and this time, I never really—no one ever made a book, to see different things that people have done. I never had a book to read or anyone to really talk about what they've been through, exactly what I'm going through, stuck in my situation. I think it's really good. I think people need help 'cause I know I sure do. I know I did back then. And you need to have something that you can go to and look at and go, "Oh, well I'm not the only one," or if you decide you're going to have an abortion, you read somebody's story and you find out what they did and how it affects them. You get to see things for exactly how they are. Anybody can tell you that something's going to be like this, but the only person that can actually share that kind of thing is someone who's actually been there, the same age.

I just want other people to know that they're not alone. Having a baby isn't going to end your life, although the TV sure makes it seem like it. The media makes us teenagers look like we can't do anything right. It depends on how you are and how you want to be—that's how you're going to be with your child. If you want to party every day, then obviously you're going to have to stop, because your first concern is supposed to be your child. I think that's the only thing that's going to make your decision a little bit different: how your lifestyle is.

My biggest fear is that I won't be a very good parent, my kids will grow up and be killers. That just pops into my mind every now and then. You need to have fear, to have worries. That's the only way you're going to make things right. If you think "this" is going to happen, you try and make sure it doesn't. You do your best, I think that's all that counts. If you do your best, then it's not your fault because you tried the best that you can. That's what I keep telling myself. It's going to be OK.

Susan

tells her

I'm eighteen. I was sixteen when I got pregnant, seventeen when I had Erica, and eighteen when I had the abortion. It's been a rough couple of years.

I met James when I was thirteen. By the time I got pregnant, we'd been together about three years and we were obviously having sex and were using birth control. We were both living at home and going to school. I was living with my mom. My parents got divorced when I was about six. I'm my mom's only child. I lived with her right up until I was about nine months pregnant. Then I moved out and now James and I live on our own.

I didn't have sex until I was fifteen. I dated James for two years before I had done it. At thirteen, my mom had explained to me what could be the consequences that come

With cigarette in hand, Susan explained how she manages the responsibilities of being a teenage mom and a devoted girlfriend, while trying to bury her guilt over an abortion.

of having sex. "If you get pregnant you might be stuck with this person for the rest of your life, if you decide to keep this child. Or you'd have to go through the emotional strain of having an abortion. Why risk anything like that, unless you're ready?" She wanted me to wait until I found some-body that I loved. She said, "Don't listen to your head, listen to your heart. If your head says go but your heart is kind of iffy about it, don't. You'll regret it. If you decide to, please talk to me first. I'll get you on birth control."

As soon as she noticed that James and I were getting closer and, I mean, the relationship had lasted a lot longer than she had expected, she said, "OK, let's go to the doctor and we'll get you on the pill." But she put me on the pill about a year before I even decided to have sex. She said, "I just want you to be prepared." So I said, "OK, whatever." I'm glad she did because, when it did happen, it was a spur-of-the-moment kind of thing. I mean, there were no condoms anywhere. I had never bought any. I had never done it before, so I was lucky that I was on the pill. My mom was really good about it, she was being realistic. She wasn't going to say, "No, wait to have sex until you're married."

When I did it for the first time, I went and told her right away. She just made me feel comfortable enough to do that. I just blurted it. I said, "Mom, I had sex with James tonight." And she goes, "And how was it?" I said, "Painful." She said, "Very painful?" I said, "Yeah." She said, "Good." She was joking around with me about it a little bit. She said, "Well, are you still on the pill? Were you using any extra protec-tion?" I said, "No." And she said, "Well, you should really try to use condoms too with the pill and make it really safe. There's nothing a hundred percent, but make it as safe as you can." I felt better because I had told her. I wasn't hiding any-thing from her. She gave me a hug before I went to bed. She was great.

I had my problem years when I was about thirteen, when I

was kind of getting into trouble and I was trying drugs a little bit and doing what my friends were doing. Everybody else was running away from home, so I thought I'd do it too, just to see what the cheap thrill was, and it was the most terrible thing I ever could have done. Before, I was actually getting good grades and all that. I never got in trouble, I was just a normal kid. It's when I moved here that I just fell into a bad crowd. They all kind of approached me and I thought that was the neatest thing. So I started getting into trouble—more out of curiosity than anything. My mom still hates me for it. I put her through a lot. I mean, I regret it.

My mom calls it my "rebellion years." We were fighting. But I mean, it was just over stupid, petty things. We didn't agree on anything. She wanted me home by nine. I figured, I'm thirteen years old, I should be allowed out until two, three in the morning. And you know, just doing chores, she would always bother me: "Do the dishes." "Well, I'll do them later." Things like that. I didn't want to listen to anything she said, she was too old. In my opinion, she had never been my age, she had no idea how I felt.

I was just a follower back then. I did all kinds of stupid, stupid things that I'll regret for the rest of my life. I ran away. I wasn't gone for long, I think it was a week at the very most. I slept in stairwells, I slept in a tree-house. Then I finally realized that home was better. I was lucky my mom always took me back. My mom was great to me.

After that I just smartened up. I think the ultimatum basically was when she told me she can't handle this any more. Either she calls the police and they deal with me, or she takes me to my aunt who lives completely in the middle of nowhere (which was devastating to me because I would be afraid to be away from all those cool friends that I had), or I go to counselling and try to work things out with her. So it didn't leave me much choice. I said I would go to counselling, and it turned out to be really good. That was a kind of new beginning for us. It was sort of respecting my mother and listening to her more. That's when things got better. Now, being a mother, I want to be just like her. I think she handled everything right. Shortly after that, I got pregnant.

What happened was, I had to go off the pill because I was getting pregnancy symptoms even though I wasn't pregnant. I was throwing up. I was sick a lot. The doctor said that the problem was that the pill was too strong, it made me feel pregnant because of the hormones in it. I had to go off it for a while, wait a month and start a new pill. In that month, we were using condoms and spermicide, and I got pregnant.

I wanted to keep her. I mean, this was my baby. I went through all the pros and cons. I guess the pros with abortion were, we could just move on and there wouldn't be a baby stopping us and we could go on with our education without any interruptions. We just could move on with our lives and be teenagers. The cons on the other side, in my eyes, it was murder. I felt like I should be put in jail if I ever did anything like that. To me it seemed like that was going to be a big emotional strain, so I decided—we decided—no to that. James feels the same way I do. He thinks the same thing, you know, if we're responsible enough to have sex, we should be responsible enough to accept any consequences that come of it. He acted as though he was pregnant too. He already had this attachment to it.

Adoption would be the same thing. There's no way he could, you know, give it to somebody else. I mean, it would have killed him. It would have killed me too. Adoption: pro again, same thing as abortion, just move on and be teenagers like we're supposed to. Keeping the baby: the pros were, we wouldn't have the cons of the other ones—murdering it or giving it away. The cons were, we wouldn't be able to move on with our lives, we'd be parents. Everything would be turned around, upside down, everything would just be haywire.

So I mean, it took a long time. There was a bunch of different things that went through our heads. Where would we live? What would we do? Would I keep going to school? Would I still be able to go to university? I called people and asked, will they have child care? James went looking for a job. When he got a job, he got health benefits with it, so I mean, that was already good.

Then we realized, OK, we would be able to pull this off. It might be tight. I said maybe I won't get an $80 pair of jeans, I might get a $30 pair. So that would mean getting the baby diapers or something. We would not mind sacrificing. That's when we decided we'll have her. That was the best thing for us.

We started having a lot of problems. We were living together, arguing all the time. I thought newborns slept. I ended up with a hyperactive baby. She didn't want to sleep, she was fighting to the end. So it was a lot more difficult than we thought it would be. The baby was so fussy all the time, and I was frustrated at the end of the day, and then he'd come home from a long day at work and he'd be frustrated and in a bad mood. Instead of telling each other, "Listen, keep your distance, I'm in a really bad mood," we'd attack each other. It was a constant attacking all the time. It wasn't at all what we expected. We didn't really talk about things.

The minute we made the baby cry because we were yelling at each other, he said, "OK, I'm leaving right now." And then he left. We broke up for about a month. It was the best thing. You know, if you make your child cry because you're arguing, it's so disrespectful to the baby. I mean, what are you doing to it? Like, what is the baby possibly thinking? So that's why we broke up. He broke up with me. He went about it saying, "I don't like you any more. You're always a grouch. Get out of my face." He tells me now it made it easier doing it that way, rather than just saying, "I can't accept the responsibility. I'm not ready for this." So he did it really badly, which just killed me. I mean, it still tears me apart just hearing the echo of his voice saying that.

That's when I got my life back on track. Before that, I was always staying home doing nothing. I didn't think babies could go outside, I didn't want her getting cold. So I was cooped up in the house all the time. When he left, I took a secretarial course. After a while I started going to school. I just realized, "OK, I lost James because I was always such a dependant, and I'm just not going to do it any more. So I might as well do something for myself." Which I did.

It's at that point that I found I was pregnant again. It was a pretty horrible thing. But my mom was there, so I was lucky. When I finally got the results, I called James at work and I told him. And he just said, "Well, OK, what are you going to do?" We weren't going out, so I guess he thought he didn't have to be there for some reason. I said, "I don't know, do you want to help me?" So then he came over and I basically just cried the whole night. And he just kind of held me there. I guess he was just shocked, like, how could this happen again?

What happened was, we hadn't had sex at all for about six weeks after Erica was born. I didn't want to, because I had lots of stitches. I had no interest in it whatsoever. The doctor said, "Wait until your next checkup." He told me not to go back on the pill until my body was back on track. When we started to have sex again, we went back to the condom and spermicide. But it made me really nervous. I told the doctor that's what I was doing when I got pregnant before. He said the chances are—I don't remember exactly what the percentages were—that that was just an unlucky break.

The doctor said, "If you want, just abstain completely." I mean, that was my thing for a long time. I just wanted James to stay away from me. Which is basically what happened for a little bit. Then we convinced ourselves that we were just unlucky, that this is probably not going to happen again. Then I used twice the amount of spermicide and the whole bit. I was really worried. Things were OK for a while. And then I went to get the pills and they said wait until the Sunday of your next period. And then Sunday passed and my period wasn't coming. I went to the doctor and said, "Listen, there's a problem, I'm not getting my period yet." He said, "Do you want a pregnancy test?" I said, "No. I don't even want to know. I already have a baby. You told me to use a condom and spermicide and that's exactly what I did. I'm not supposed to be pregnant." He said, "OK, we'll wait another week." I was just like, OK. I'm just sitting here and I'm praying, "Oh, God, please, please."

I went back a week later. He did a pregnancy test and, sure enough, it happened again. Which was mind-blowing because, I mean, how could it possibly happen to me twice? He said that up until six months after you've had a baby, you're like a walking time-bomb, you can get pregnant because of all the hormones that are still running through your body. So I should have just abstained completely. Had I known, I wouldn't have had sex, period. I was breast-feeding, so your period's not supposed to come. The doctor told me something about that. He said when women are breast-feeding they are less likely to get pregnant. But don't rely on that as any type of birth control.

I was about six weeks pregnant when James and I talked about it. If I didn't want to have an abortion, he was going to do his best to support the second baby. I said I wanted to keep it. We discussed if we could possibly do it financially. I mean, it was only a two-bedroom attic apartment. He works two jobs and he gets paid pretty well, but living conditions would've been terrible. We get a break on our rent. We live upstairs in his uncle's house. We only pay $300 a month rent. The rooms are small enough as it is. Two kids in one room would've been like living in a closet. I think that's wrong. Kids like to play around.

Erica was still going to be in her crib, so where were we going to put the other one? How was I possibly going to take care of both? I think we were discussing more as parents, how would we provide for the kids? It did come up about our relationship a little bit. I told him that we have to be clear that we're not going out. We're not together. I said, "Do you think it's right? Are you going to be there for your kid? You're there for Erica, are you going to be there for this one too?" Then he started arguing, "Well of course I'm going to be there! What do you think?"

Erica was already here—she was alive, she was born, she was sleeping in her crib—while this second one's probably just got its heartbeat. It wasn't even really considered human yet. So we had to think about the one that was already born, the one that we were already providing for. If we did have this child, what would we be taking away from Erica? I wanted to give her the best; I didn't want to take away from both of them. Neither did James.

So that's when we slowly realized there was no way we could possibly have two kids and provide for both of them. That was the hardest thing for me to do. It was going against everything I believed in. Abortion, to me, is murder. But I don't think I had a choice. We were so tight with one kid already. I was going nowhere with my life. I was stuck at home like a housewife at eighteen years old. I had to go to school to make something of myself. I had to get a job. I never could have paid to put two kids in day care. I probably wouldn't have been able to go back to school. I didn't want to have to go on welfare. I have a lot of pride. I don't think taxpayers should have to pay for my kids. Most teenage mothers don't have a choice, but in my case, I did.

My mom works at a church, and I remember going in one day and I found this Catholic Church kind of brochure. It actually showed a baby that had been aborted at six months old, and I mean, I was flabbergasted seeing that. This little human in a bucket. It explained all about how it had been taken out and I just freaked. I showed my mom. She explained to me that that's the procedure. I wasn't pregnant then, so I didn't realize that you could feel the baby moving around by then. I said, "Well, if you know the baby's alive, how could you possibly kill it? This is something you made." And that was my cue. That's why it became like murder to me. It's totally immoral.

Adoption, I just couldn't do. I mean, feeling a baby growing inside me, get bigger, feeling it kick and hearing it hiccup and things like that, I could never, never have done that.

The day after we realized that we were going to choose abortion, I started calling around to all the hospitals and clinics to find out where and when I could have an abortion done. I made an appointment. First I had to go to a preoperative appointment and they checked me out, made sure everything was OK. They needed to see how far along I was and set up an appointment to have this tent inserted. It's a tent that they put in your cervix the day before an abortion, so that the cervix dilates naturally. They then don't have to use medical instruments to open the cervix to remove the foetus. That way they don't risk doing any damage to you. It was painful.

The appointment was at some office I'd never been to, with a doctor that I'd never met before. He watched me come in with my daughter. I couldn't just leave her at home, I had to bring her with me. I look younger than I am, people think I'm thirteen, fourteen years old. So the doctor's thinking I'm that young, with a baby, and I'm aborting another. I did not like this doctor. I just felt like he kept judging me, like I was some kind of slut. I thought to myself, "You discover a method of birth control that's one hundred percent and I'll use it. Until then, don't judge me."

The first thing he said was, "Why didn't you use protection?" So I just looked at him and said, "And who are you? This isn't any of your business. I'm here for one reason. You're here for one reason. Now do your job and don't ask me any questions." He didn't say anything to me after that, he just explained the procedure. I don't know exactly what words he was using, but I said to him, "So you're going to go into my uterus and scrape everything that's in there out, then use a vacuum to get it out. So basically you're going to be ripping this kid out of me." He said, "Well, if you want to put it like that, yes." I was thinking, oh my god, I might as well be put into that brochure that I saw two years earlier, with my baby in the bucket, and that hurt me. I was picturing all this when I started thinking that they're going to hurt me somehow, because he had said that there's risks involved. He told me when and where to go for the operation, which would be in a week.

I was really nervous. I was thinking about all the things that could go wrong and maybe this wasn't the right decision or the right choice. I was just really nervous. I talked to my mom a whole lot. I was glad she was there as much as she was. The day of the abortion, I was pretty nervous and fidgety. You had to put on that stupid gown and fill out a bunch of forms. I was just flipping really quickly through magazines. Then the doctor that I don't like came to take me in. My mom gave me a hug and a kiss and said, "Good luck, everything will be fine." Then she took Erica back to the waiting-room.

We went into this huge room, it looked like something out of "The X-Files." It was really bare, with this bed in the middle. Next to it was all the surgical instruments. There was all these nurses and they gave me an IV and then put this mask on my face and told me to count down from one hundred. As I was counting down, I was looking at the instruments, and the last thought that I can remember was, "I'm not having any of that anywhere near me. I cannot do this to my kid." I remember trying to get up. If I had had five more seconds, I could have taken the mask off and gotten up and walked out.

The next thing that I remember, I was in the recovery room, and for some strange reason the first thing that I did was check to see if I was bleeding. The doctor had explained to me that there would be blood after the abortion. There was blood all over my fingers. That's when I started to cry. The nurse came and asked me if I was OK. She asked me if I wanted some Tylenol. I said, "Tylenol isn't going to do it, my heart is breaking." She said, "I apologize. Sometimes we get reactions like this." Meanwhile there's all these other girls walking around and laughing, and I'm thinking to myself, what is your problem, look at what you just did. I was just crying and crying. My mom came in and she hugged me and gave me Erica. It always makes me feel better to see her, to hug her.

The feeling that I had at that time—the emptiness, road-kill, worthless—just never left. It hasn't gone away at all. I just feel terrible. The guilt is overwhelming. I never imagined I would be feeling all the things that I'm feeling now. I thought I would be upset, then I'd get over it. But it's been months now and I'm nowhere near getting over it. I feel the same way today as I did the day I woke up in the recovery room. I just felt so empty. That empty has been there ever since.

The whole thing was a horrible emotional strain, to have an abortion. I just feel so many mixed feelings: shock, pain, confusion, frustration, not knowing what to do. I'm just so lucky that I have so much support from everywhere. My mom helps me a little bit, James helps as much as he can, but I think that I have to help myself. Whenever I start thinking about all this I start to cry, smoke a whole lot, bite all my fingernails off. I get nervous and tense.

It's complicated. It's horrible. My mom always told me I came from the angels, and when kids look down from the sky they see their mom and dad. They pick them and then they're conceived. The way I think about it, this kid was in a hurry and wanted me to be its mom. What I did was tell it to wait up in heaven until I'm ready. That's the only way I could possibly deal with it, or else I would just break down.

I don't have sex with my boyfriend any more. I don't want him near me at all, I don't want him touching me, I don't even like kissing him. He's like a germ. I'm totally turned off by it. It's sex in general, I don't want it. James just happens to be the guy that I'm with, so he's the unlucky one who doesn't get anything. Once in a while I'll kiss him on the mouth, but I don't get butterflies in my stomach any more. It's just dead. It tortures me to say, "Don't touch me," because I love him with all my heart and I know he loves me too, but he can't understand. I'm afraid I'm going to lose him. I feel like I'm losing everything because of what happened. I lost this baby, I might be losing James. All because of a wrong decision. I didn't know this was going to happen. I just don't want him to leave. I love him so much, I don't want him to go.

We did try one time to have sex. I thought, OK, I'll make the effort, maybe it won't be as bad as I think. We had condoms, spermicide and the pill. But it got to me so bad that sex was actually physically hurting me. I was tensing up and I said, "Get off me," and I went into the bathroom and cried. It was horrible. It was like I was getting raped. All that was going through my head was, "You're going to get pregnant again, you're going to have to have an abortion again, you're going to commit murder. You're going to rot in hell." There was just no possible way that I could enjoy it with all these things going through my head.

I told my mom about the hurting part. She said that maybe instead of it being physical, it's psychological, but she's not a psychiatrist. That's why I'm going to start counselling. I'm wondering if it'll ever go away or is it going to be like this for the rest of my life. I'm just so afraid of getting pregnant again. If I do, I know I'll keep it. I don't care what happens, because I couldn't go through the emotional pain of having an abortion again.

I don't talk about this to my mother or James. I don't think they would understand how rough it is, they haven't gone through it. Sometimes people tell me it's harder to have an abortion after you've had a kid because, if you don't have kids, you don't know what it's like to have one. Erica's the most precious thing to me, ever. I would die for her. Then I have this other kid and I kill it so that I don't have to make any more sacrifices in my life. I probably could have taken care of it, because I'm a hell of a good mother—well, to Erica. But to this kid I'm the worst mother that could ever exist. It's such a contradiction.

Sometimes I feel guilty when I'm with Erica. I might get annoyed with something little, like she's throwing her food around, and I think, oh my god, I'm being a terrible mother. It's all these over-reactions I have. I feel ashamed a lot faster than I did when she was younger. I know it's odd. I'm just so paranoid that I'm being a terrible mother to her too. In our apartment in the winter, it's cold, and if I get mad that she's woken me up when I'm having a good dream, I'll end up crying because I feel so guilty and so ashamed that I've gotten mad at her. I don't know why she won't sleep through the night like other people's babies. I know there's no reason to feel guilty or ashamed. All parents have these momentary thoughts, there's nothing wrong with them.

Everything that I first thought was right ended up feeling so wrong after. I thought I was making the right decision. Maybe I could have worked harder. I feel like I was working my butt off, but maybe I was being selfish. I could have made more sacrifices. I feel so low—a terrible person, a horrible mother. The kid didn't ask to be brought into this world, or be conceived in the first place, then I have to put it through torture to make it go away.

This abortion has made me want to work twice as hard at everything. At school, I'm trying to get extra-good grades so I can get an extra-good job so I can provide even more for Erica and save up for when I'm ready to bring my other baby back down from heaven. I'm taking correspondence courses. They take, on average, six months to complete; I just completed one in three weeks. I'm constantly working. I'm straining myself. I don't sleep. I have bad dreams. I dream about walking out of the operating-room. When I wake up, I'm depressed again.

I don't think abortion is completely wrong. For some people it might be what they have to do. Maybe they can't provide for a child in any way and, like in my case, they were using birth control and got pregnant by accident. Then maybe the right decision for that person is abortion or adoption. If my daughter came to me and said she was pregnant, I would tell her that I would support and respect any decision she makes about the pregnancy. Whatever she wants, I'll do everything I can to help her. I just want her to make the decision that she feels is best for her and her baby. I was taught all the right values by my mom and I'm going to do my best to teach my daughter all the right values too.

■

I think I'm doing this interview because I'm trying to make myself feel better, to talk about all my feelings. I think sometimes it's easier to tell all your feelings to a complete stranger than to someone you love very much. I do feel better after having said all this, especially since a lot of it I've never said before.

Guianna

tells her

 STORY

My name is Guianna. I'm seventeen years old. The first guy I
dated would have been when I was just about to turn sixteen.
It wasn't thought about really, but it was safe, meaning we
used a condom. I ended up seeing this guy for seven months
and then I broke up with him. About half a year later I
started going out with Dave, and about three months later we
started sleeping together. I was on the pill and we were using
a condom for the most part, but the pill was having weird
effects on my body and I got depressed and I got lots of
headaches. I tried four different kinds and they didn't work
and I didn't feel normal.

*Over french fries and tea,
Guianna told me about her
pregnancy, which she
aborted six months prior to
our interview. She revealed
the details of her relationship with her boyfriend,
her plans for school and
her dream to travel around
the world.*

I got the pills at the health clinic.
They were very helpful there. Once
you say you want to go on the pill,
they sit you down for about two
hours and show you every single
other option you could possibly
have, including celibacy. They don't
try to convince you not to go on the
pill. You end up paying about five
bucks a month for the pills.

Then I went off the pill and we were using condoms. I had just finished having my period, so we thought we didn't need to use a condom this time. Then the next day we would use it and then sometimes we wouldn't in the heat of the moment. Neither of us would say anything about it. Afterwards, both of us would be like, "Dumb, dumb, dumb." But it would just keep happening. That's how it happened. We were just saying, well, we'll stop for about five days in between and we were both just being real irresponsible about it. I'm not usually that irresponsible, but I guess I was just not thinking. Then we'd use this method—I don't remember what it's called—yeah, the rhythm method. So we did that. It was dumb. I hated myself after a couple of times. So then, finally, I missed my period and for two weeks we were sort of stalling, like, "No! No! You're not pregnant." And I would say, "Yeah, I am, I know my body. This isn't normal. I know I am."

We talked about it, but it was firmly set in my mind that if it happened and I got pregnant, then I would get an abortion. There was no question of what would be done. I didn't think I could do adoption. I didn't think I could go to the full term and give birth to a child and then give it away. I would just get too attached to it—being as how attached I got to this, you know, in ten weeks. Attached enough to wonder if abortion was the right thing to do. Sometimes I would be fine with it and think, "This was a stupid mistake on my and my boyfriend's part. There is no reason to ruin the child's life or my life by having a baby right now."

I fantasized about being a mom but not about being a mom right now. I couldn't fathom it: seventeen years old, finishing high school and then what? Giving birth to a child and then doing what? Living with my parents and raising a child in their house? I didn't have enough money to do anything. Before it happened, I was very set in my pro-choice. I almost didn't even see the other side of the coin. At this age, why would you keep a child who you can't afford? At the same time there was something exciting about it too. Wow! I didn't really think this could happen or I would have been more careful.

We went to the health clinic. I got a urine test. Then the lady, her name was Francine, came back and she said, "Yes, you are pregnant," and I felt really calm about it at the time. It didn't come as a surprise at all. Francine was very calm about it. She said, "Here's some information. You already told me you wanted an abortion if this happened. Here's the support you might need." Then we just had to decide on where to go and what kind of procedure to use. Francine gave me fact sheets on different clinics around the city, places to have abortions. They had all been rated for comfort, bedside manner, that type of thing. I knew of someone who'd had an abortion. She had gone to this clinic and found it to be very good. It had one of those high comfortability ratings, so I thought OK, that sounds good. I wanted to be in the warmest, nicest place possible, so that's the place that we picked.

I put on weight and my breasts got bigger. I actually thought it was kind of neat. I thought it was pretty interesting. Sometimes it felt really good, like, wow, I can really do this! It was around this point that I started feeling very sick. I must have been three or four weeks pregnant. I smoked before and now just the smell of cigarettes from one person walking by across the street would make me feel like puking. I would just feel so nauseous. I started feeling depressed.

Then I started to feel guilt. I was pretty down on myself. I couldn't believe that I had actually let this happen. I didn't know who I was going to tell, who I should tell.

I was very selective about telling my friends. It's not that I didn't think they'd be supportive, I just felt bad about myself. I felt they would see it as carelessness on my part. They weren't like that at all. Half of my friends hadn't discussed this with anyone before. They hadn't been in a relationship longer than three months. It was too much to deal with, like if someone in your family or in someone else's family dies, you'd only be able to say, "I'm here for you if you need me." But you've never been in that situation yourself and you don't know what to do, you don't know how to help. That's the way it was for my friends. They said, "If you want me to go with you or if you need someone to talk to..." At the time, it just didn't feel like enough at all. I felt like I was going through something completely hellish. There was no one I could turn to for help or even just to talk to. When I think about it now, I don't know what kind of reaction I wanted people to have. I guess I wanted them to have more of one because in my life it was this huge thing I had to deal with every single day. For a long time there were these feelings of abandonment by my friends, but they weren't abandoning me. I just wanted someone to do something, to come over and to say, "It's OK. Here, Guianna, have some flowers" or something. I wanted someone to physically show that they cared rather than just saying stuff like, "I'm here when you need me." And me wanting to say, "I need you all the time. I need you right now. Can you be here right now?" I wouldn't say that. Maybe I was too proud. I'd say, "OK, when I need you, I'll call." But I wouldn't, because I'd just feel silly.

I would feel like crying because I was pregnant. I'd wake up in the morning feeling sick to my stomach. I would feel sick in my classes all day long knowing that something was growing inside my stomach that I didn't choose to be there, knowing that I had to go through this horrible procedure to get it out. Having my friends know that I was going through this and sitting beside me laughing and joking—it just felt so trivial. I realize it is too much to expect from other people, but at the time that's how I felt, this overwhelming feeling that nobody cares.

I ended up taking it all out on my boyfriend and just screaming at him. I didn't know what I said to him half that time. I thought it was bad afterwards about the way I treated him, because I just screamed at him. I had nowhere else to take everything out—all the sadness and guilt and anger and frustration. He didn't like it at all. But he also felt guilty, because he's a good guy and he felt most upset. I don't think he ever felt more responsible for anything in his life. He was totally supportive for the whole time. He didn't know where to turn to for his frustrations because he didn't feel he could take them out on me, the way I was doing on him; he felt that I was under so much pressure. People would come up to me to see how I was doing, but nobody came up to him to see how he was doing. He was feeling all this pain and saying, "Don't think I don't feel terrible as well." I overlooked that a lot. I didn't realize what an emotional thing it was for him. All I saw was that I was going through it, not him. He made me click in sometimes: "You're not the only one, I did play some part in this. I do care about you and this is not some trivial little thing for me. Don't think it doesn't weigh on my mind. It does." So that helped. Sometimes he'd get really mad

and say, "I can't take this any more. I can't take you screaming at me all the time." And then I'd calm down and say,
"You're right. I'm sorry for taking it all out on you. I just
don't know where else to turn." I was just so frustrated. I felt
like crap for two months. Sleeping was the only thing
remotely comforting.

At that point I felt terrible. I didn't want to leave my
house. I didn't want to go anywhere or do anything. I just
wanted to be sick and cry, which is what I did most of the
time. I just bawled my eyes out. I don't know how my parents
didn't notice. Once, I was in the kitchen with my mom and
we were just talking about things. I started eating pickles and
I didn't realize how many I was eating. Then she said, "Look
how many pickles you've eaten. The last time I did that was
when I was pregnant." So I put the jar away and she never
said anything about it afterwards.

I had horrible dreams. You could get a choice of going
under full anaesthetic or partial anaesthetic. The only places
that offered full anaesthetic were hospitals and I didn't want
to do it in a hospital. It seemed like such a cold atmosphere to
me, but I was deciding, yeah, full anaesthetic, 'cause then I
could just black out. But then I'd have dreams where I'd have
full anaesthetic and I'd wake up and the doctors would have
done something weird, something way more than they were
supposed to: I couldn't have kids, I didn't have all the right
parts any more. This made me decide not to go under full
anaesthetic. Then I would have other dreams where I was
under partial anaesthetic. I would be awake and the doctors
would be doing some kind of surgery to me and it would be
wrong, it was not what they were supposed to be doing. I
would be watching them and I couldn't tell them to stop. I

couldn't say, "No, you can't do this to me." I could just stare at them blankly 'cause I was half under this anaesthetic. These dreams were horrible. I'd wake up scared stiff that this was actually going to happen to me.

I had the abortion right after spring break. I think I was ten weeks by the time I had it. I didn't eat anything the day before at all. I remember going to classes in the morning, but I don't remember being conscious of them. I wasn't really sad, I wasn't really anything, I was just waiting for two o'clock to roll around. I went to my first class and then skipped off my second class and went with a friend for coffee. I didn't drink anything. She smoked and I asked her not to, it made me feel sick. I don't remember if she talked to me much. She was very worried, but she didn't try to hold my hand or anything. I just wanted it to be over, to get there.

Dave and I took the subway down. We both didn't say much. I was walking really slowly getting there. My brain was turned off. I was numb. They gave me an address for the place and that was it. There was no sign outside that said *Clinic*. At first that made me feel on edge, but then I realized why they had done it this way—because they had been picketed before. Abortion clinics have been blown up or bombed before. It makes sense that they would have this much protection. Once I thought about it, it made me feel safer, because they were taking these kinds of precautions to make sure that the place was protected, and also it's much more confidential that way.

The people at the clinic were really nice to me. But the whole time Dave was sitting beside me in the waiting-room, I didn't want him to be there. I didn't want him touching me, I didn't want him to give me a hug. I didn't want him to come near me at all. All of the time during the ten weeks, there were a lot of times that he would come to give me a hug and I would stiffen up. It wasn't just him, I wouldn't want any-body to come near me, to come too close. Sometimes it would make me feel nauseous, a claustrophobic-type nauseousness. It was so weird, because the more I think about it, the more it seems the emotions were contradictory. Sometimes I wanted him there, sometimes I didn't want him to touch me.

The whole day of the abortion, I just felt delirious. I didn't know what was going on. I did physically, but in my head I didn't want to think about it any more, I wanted it all to be over. I wanted it to have been a dream. It was nerve-racking sitting in a room with all these other people, guys and girls. I was wondering if they felt the same way that I did. I don't think I even made eye contact with any of them. I don't think any of them made eye contact with each other. We all just had our heads down. I tried not to think about what I was actually doing. I wanted to detach myself from it, brain-wise. I didn't want to think, "You're having an abortion. You're killing something that is alive in some form." Me and Dave— you might call it coyish—we wouldn't even call it a baby. We would say "it" so we wouldn't make any sort of attachments that would feel bad later.

I had to sign a few things: a release form, and medical-insurance-type forms. They say it is all confidential; over sixteen, your parents never have to find out anything about it. One nurse talked to me a little bit about the anaesthesia. She gave me a sheet with the side-effects of what bad things could happen. I read it without trying to think about any of them. I thought, I'll just sign the form and not back out now.

When we went in to see the doctor, seeing that it was a

guy was shocking. He seemed a nice guy, but any internal exam I'd had was done by a female, so it seemed really odd that this man was doing it. He did an ultrasound and he was talking to me the whole time. He was very polite about everything, he wasn't rude, he had a good manner about him. Finally, it was time to go upstairs where they did the abortions. I was looking at Dave as I was leaving, and I said, "See you in a couple of hours. OK, bye." He told me afterwards that he couldn't sit still. He went to a coffee shop and ate donuts and bagels and lots of food.

When I was upstairs, they found I have very small veins, so they couldn't put an IV in my arm. It started to freak me out, and I got tense. Finally they got one in. So I'm lying there with my arm straight out and it felt really uncomfortable. They put in needles to anaesthetize the area, I guess, or to make it dilate. That was really painful. They said it would only be ten or fifteen minutes, but it seemed like it was a lot longer. It felt terrible. It was really painful. Two female nurses—I was squeezing their hands really tight. I felt terrible the whole time it was going on. I was trying to smile, trying to be, like, "It's OK, it's what you have to do." They were all really nice. They were talking the whole time, asking me questions. The doctor asked me what I want to do with my life. I have a small tattoo of a star on my thigh and he mentioned that. I still think it was better than someone who didn't say anything. It was the whole concept of it: the doctor and all these instruments. The whole thing, the vacuum—just the sound of it was really horrible. The noise, the idea of it inside of me was terrifying. The noise amplified my feelings of it. It was like terror. I was thinking that I was killing something, being sucked out of me without any...I still think about it now. Who knows what piece of that is still around in the world right now? Meaning that whatever they do with whatever they suck out of you—it seems so mechanical. I don't even know how to put it, how I feel about it.

When it was done I felt empty. I could feel there was emptiness. I don't know if it was more mental than physical. It felt weird to walk, really awkward. They immediately change your underwear, if you brought in other underwear. They gave me a pad. They walked me out to the lounge chair. They gave me a nice hot-water bottle. They gave me cookies and, if I wanted tea or juice or water or milk, I just had to ask. They were really nice, they were making sure I was OK. I had to stay there for at least an hour, or longer. I didn't fall asleep, I was just lying there, feeling really good not having to deal with anything. Nobody was talking to me. At one point they asked me to go to the bathroom and take off the pad and put it in the garbage. Then they would come and look what colour the blood was, to see if everything was fine. And everything was.

The whole thing took an hour and a half. I got dressed and went downstairs. Dave was standing there all white. His eyes were bugging out of his head. At that point it was more of a relief to see him, just to have someone there. He asked me exactly what happened. We were going to take a cab to my house, and he was going to stay the night and give my parents any number of excuses for it. We ended up just walking home really slowly, 'cause I couldn't walk quickly, that hurt a little. I just wanted to feel able to walk. I didn't want to feel pampered. It wasn't that far from my house, just a half-hour walk. We were talking and joking more. Just being lighthearted about it. It's over. It's gone. I wanted to get on with things.

People called me that night. "How was it? Are you OK? Did everything go well?" I said it went well, it was really painful but I'm OK. I slept. I was really tired. It was pretty painful for the next while. I went to school the next day. I was still feeling very down, but my head felt a little lighter: "OK, well, it's done now, I can't do anything about it." I felt a little bit of relief, but not till about a month later, when I stopped bleeding.

The people at the clinic said that in a couple of weeks I'd go through a really big mood swing. I didn't go through any big mood swing, but then in a month, I woke up one morning, I felt great. I felt so good. I felt like I was out of a tunnel. "Wow! I just went through three months of hell and it's over. It's done. It's behind me now and I'm OK with myself and with everything—I'm fine." I felt so much better.

Afterward, when I was totally through it, I told my friends how I had felt, how I wished they had been there, that they had done something. One of my friends started bawling. She was, like, "I didn't know. I'm so sorry that I wasn't there. I didn't know that's how bad you felt. I don't know how you can ever forgive me. You've been going through this hell for three months and I didn't even know." She was just so upset. It felt really good telling some of my friends about it. I wanted them to know. Maybe it's not how they'll feel if they ever go through it. Hopefully this will be some kind of lesson so they don't have to go through it. I know that, in comparison to a lot of the people I know, I am strong in the sense that things that have happened in my life with my parents and with this—I've just gone through it and came out the other side and been able to go on with things.

Hopefully, it won't happen again. It's not something that everyone should go through. But to have gone through it changed my outlook on a lot of things. This whole time, for those three months, I was going through my last year of high school. I ended up doing well in school. I also had a part-time job. I've been a very independent person my whole life, with money and stuff, I've been working since Grade 9. People would say, "Oh god, Guianna, it sounds so hard to do all your courses for college. And you're doing it in four years instead of five!" But that wasn't the hard part of my year, you know. That part was easy. It just made me more confident in my ability to deal with things. If something bad happens to me these days, I just think how much worse it could be, because it has been, so I can deal with it now. I feel it was something that happened in my life and there is no denying it. I went through it and that's it. Now I know I'll be more careful.

My sex life changed when I knew that I was pregnant. I don't think sex was nearly as good. There was some sense of, "This is what got me to where I am right now." It didn't feel the way it normally feels. That would sort of weird me out: the thought that I could be hurting myself, hurting something inside me, along with feeling guilty about having to do that anyway. We didn't end up having a very sexual relationship during that time at all. We did sometimes, but not often. Then, for that month afterward, when I was bleeding for a month, I didn't want him to come near me. Even after I sort of felt better about everything, I really did not want it to happen again. I was really scared. It took a while before we started sleeping together again. We were kissing and hugging, but that was it. I didn't feel comfortable with anything else. When we did start to have sex again, I would stop and feel frightened that it would happen again. I was on the pill again, a different kind that they gave me right after the abortion.

Then I felt that the relationship started to feel too claustrophobic. So I broke with him about a month after that. We were planning to go away. I wanted to see all my friends and I wanted to hang out with them a lot before I went away. He just thought that I was with them too much, that I wasn't spending any time with him. In a way, he was right. I had just distanced myself from him a lot. Whether it was because of the abortion or just because I was falling out of love with him, I'm not sure. I felt that the relationship had stopped working. I still love him and miss him. He's gone away now. But we stayed on good terms.

I wasn't born in Canada. I was born in the Ukraine. I was two years old when I came here. My parents were new immigrants. Both my parents grew up in harsh, different conditions from the ones I grew up in. Their lives were so much tougher than mine. I think they are very open-minded people. It's just me, my mom and my dad. I have a half-sister and a half-brother who are from my dad's previous marriage. My dad and my mom split up for a year and I lived with my mom. I was much happier living with just my mom because me and my dad don't get along, to the point where just to spend ten minutes in a room together we would get into a huge screaming argument because I disagree with just about everything he has to say. He's very racist in my eyes, and homophobic. If I ask him to give me a drive to the subway, he just picks on me as if I was the most unappreciative person in the world. It gets to me, because he won't do stuff for me at all. I always say to them, "I'm never going to ask you guys for anything. I'm always going to do things for myself. I don't want your help." When I do ask for things from them, my mom's OK, but my dad gives me the biggest hassle in the world. My mom got fed up and they separated, but finally my mom agreed to come back.

I want to go to university next year. I've been saving up money myself, and my parents set up a scholarship fund for me as soon as they came here. It matures when I turn eighteen. It's a really good sum to go to school with, in combination with money I'll have saved by then. Soon, I'm quitting my job and taking off, probably for at least a year. I've been planning to travel for ever and a half. Since I was really small, I've wanted to go to the Amazon, to the rain forest.

I was thinking during the abortion that my mom had an abortion after we came to Canada when I was two years old. They just didn't have enough money to afford to have another child. And after that, she couldn't have any kids. She kept having miscarriages over and over again. I haven't been checked out yet by a doctor. I don't know why I haven't gotten up the courage to go. I think my mother's experience caused me to have some doubts. But I'm pretty confident that the procedure was fine and that I'm OK. Maybe I should go get it checked out and find out for sure.

I don't regret my decision. It was a necessity. But I wouldn't want anybody to ever have to go through it, because I've never felt so horrible in my life for so long. I've been in holes before, but never in holes I didn't think I'd ever get out of. I didn't think that the feelings I had then would end, how terrible I felt would ever go away. Then that day when I finally felt better, it really was like coming out of a tunnel. And that was it. I guess that's it.

Samantha

tells her
STORY

I'm nineteen, I'm already a mother. My son's name is Daval. He's three years old. It's a crazy story. He's a child that shouldn't have been born.

I was fifteen turning sixteen. I was walking home from swimming class, like I always did. There's a walkway that you have to walk along to get to my house. I'd walked that path so many times, it's not like I was scared or thought that anything was going to happen to me. I was just walking home. I was wearing my Walkman.

I remember my head getting hit, and then hitting the ground. That's about all I remember. I never saw him. At first I thought I got robbed, because my Walkman was gone. When I got up I was feeling a lot of pain. When I got home I clued in. I knew what happened when I went into the bathroom. There was a lot of blood and a lot of scratches on my face. I waited for a while and then I started to cry. A lot. I sat on the

Samantha sat across from me, hands in her lap and feet on the table. With confidence, drive and a hint of anger she relayed the details of her rape, the resulting pregnancy, her choice to keep the baby, and the consequences.

edge of the bathtub. My sister came in after a while. She looked to me and whispered, "What happened?" I started to cry. She looked at me and whispered, "Who did this to you?" I didn't answer. She asked me again. I just kept crying. Finally, with my nods and stuff, I guess, she figured it out.

I found out I was pregnant four months afterwards. I didn't know what being pregnant felt like. I just thought it was because of the stress. The rape itself was a nightmare. To find out I was pregnant now just meant it hadn't ended.

They said, "You're pregnant," and I said, "OK, I'm going to kill it." To me it wasn't a child, it was an alien. Devil Spawn. That's the way I thought of it. I had no sympathy, I was going to kill it. I don't believe in abortion in my life. I don't believe in it as a means of birth control. If it's life and death, then I believe in it. I believe rape is life and death. I was supposed to have an abortion, but with my body, if I'd had an abortion, I wouldn't have been able to have kids again and that would make me feel really terrible. I'm the kind of person that is very giving and very loving and I wanted to have a child that I could give everything to. That was my belief and that was my feeling. It was a very hard decision based on the fact that I was still at home, living with my parents, and basically it was, "I have this child or I never have kids again." People said I was too young, but I thought I was mature enough to make that decision, so I did.

My parents were like, "You're not having this child." They were really upset. Extremely. My mother wouldn't talk to me. My father was constantly down my throat because of it, and finally one day I just said, "Look, I'm leaving." I went to a shelter for quite a while. I have a cousin who was already at the shelter. My dad would send me money.

I was in school up until they told me I couldn't go. I was eight and a half months pregnant. I was going to therapy three times a week with the school counsellor. I hadn't talked to anyone, so it was good to talk. I accepted that I was pregnant and I was going to have this child. I thought about adoption, but to carry a child for nine months and then go through labour, you can't go through that and then give it away.

When he was born, I flipped. He was half white! I'm not a racist person, don't get me wrong, but I didn't expect it. I didn't know the rapist was white until my son was born. It shocked me. I definitely didn't expect that. Four hundred years of pain of black people and white people. I'm very well educated on my black history, and I'm proud of it. And I got raped by a white man, and I was pissed. Royally pissed.

For the first three days I didn't even want to look at him, I was so angry. I refused to breast-feed. I wouldn't hold him. I think what worked was, the day I got home I had an appointment with my psychiatrist. She sat me down and said, "You can blame this three-day-old baby for what happened four hundred years ago, or what happened nine months ago, or you can look at him and realize that half of him is you. Half of that baby is you." So it was like a shot of reality.

It took a while, but the first smile, the first wink, the first laugh, the first giggle...you start watching this child do things, you're amazed. If you sit and watch the child for twenty minutes, that's real entertainment. It's a mind-blow. He turned out to be a pretty cute kid, too. He had blue eyes and reddish-brown hair. He was beautiful.

When he was about two months old, he woke me up one morning. He was hungry, but he was quiet about it. He wasn't screaming or whining or anything. He was just in his crib babbling. So I went over. I looked over the side of the crib and he looked up at me and started smiling and laughing, and I thought, "Ohhhh, you're so cute." From that day he was my child. Definitely my child. He was my prized possession. Still is.

Everybody thinks it's cool to have kids: "Oh, you got a little baby." But it's not like a doll or anything like that. It's a lot of responsibility. It's really difficult. You've got to rely on a lot of different people. If a teenager comes to me now and tells me they could do it on their own, they're crazy, because it's very difficult, financially, mentally and emotionally.

I think I had it harder than a lot of other mothers because of questions like, "Who's the father?" and you're like...I don't know. It's not like I can pinpoint one person and say, "He's the father." Another thing staged a large problem for me because it posed a lot of questions for a lot of people. They'd say, "He's half white. Why? Who's the father?" And then you can't say, "Well, the father is a rapist." At that point I think, "What am I going to tell this child when he is older? What am I going to say to him?" I don't know what to say to him. When he's older and says, "Who's my father?" I don't know what to say. You can't explain that to a child. It would crush a child.

After Daval was born, my parents still weren't talking to me. So basically I had the shelter, aunts and uncles that did a great job, friends and stuff like that. I just tried to maintain sanity. I still hadn't quite gotten rid of my gung-ho youth, my wild side. I still wanted to do all the things that I did before: getting into fights, just hanging out. That's what I wanted to do, but I had this child. I know a lot of people thought negative of it and one actually thought it was pretty stupid that I continued to do what I always wanted to do. I'm a very strong-headed person. There were a lot of different events where people would say they were going to call a child protection agency on me because I wasn't a good enough mother. Basically I told them to go stick their nose somewhere else, to put it politely. And I didn't really care.

It got to a point where I wasn't mistreating him, I wasn't beating him or not taking care of him, but one time it was two o'clock in the morning and I'm outside with a baby stroller and people were looking at me like I was crazy. I took care of him but still wanted to do what I wanted to do, and I think that was very wrong of me, very selfish. I was mature, but I wasn't mature enough to know that the responsibility of a child is a lot more than having him, feeding him, changing him and that's it. There's a lot more to it. You have to give your child respect. You don't have a two-month-old, three-month-old, even two-year-old baby out at two o'clock in the morning. There's no reason for that. A child needs to feel

protected at all times. You can't do that when you're down-town, outside, and around people who are smoking or doing whatever else.

My mom used to say, "Once you have a child, your life is over and their life begins. You're living your life to make your child's life better," and I wasn't doing that. I was still trying to live my life at the same time. You can live your life, but your life is supposed to change. You're supposed to grow more mature and pay more attention to your responsibilities, and I wasn't doing that.

He started to walk. That was the good news. He started to walk and babble and laugh. I had my own place. Things got a lot better. I was working. My parents were more trusting, more compassionate towards me. They would help with the baby-sitting.

I stayed with Daval for about a year, then I started work-ing again. I'd give him to my parents. They'd take him. Then things started to get really hard. I started working longer hours to afford where I was living and to afford to buy clothes. So he spent more time at my parents' house, which my mother loved. She got more attached to him. Basically he was living at my parents' house because I was working hours that I was up at seven-thirty a.m. to get to work for ten a.m. I'd work all hours of the night, until all the work was done. We'd close at nine-thirty p.m., then it would take about one hour to count the money and restock the shelves. So basically I was seeing my child about three hours a day, and my mother didn't approve of that. That went on until he was about two. But I couldn't quit my job. I was trying to pay bills, support him with money—have money to do the things...give him the things he deserves. By the time I realized that something was wrong, it was too late, my mother already...About three weeks after he turned two and a half, she told me, "I'm taking him from you." And I was just like, "What do you mean?"

Now, my parents are well off. My parents have it made. I can't say that it was handed to them on a silver platter, because it wasn't. They worked really hard to get it, but they've got it now. My parents could give him anything he wanted. He could say he wanted a car and my parents could give it to him, and I couldn't do that. Well, it became one really big court battle, and my mother pulled up dirt that I never even knew that she knew. The child protection agency got involved.

Basically, the moral of the story is, I lost my son to my parents. The court took away something that was mine. He was part of me. My mother now has my son. She's had him for about six months. I have no contact with them at all. My mother and I don't speak. We can't stand each other. I won't subject my child to fist-fights. I won't let him see violence. And if me and my mother are in the same room, there'll be violence. I'd kill her if she put her hands on my child. And if my child calls her "mother," that's even worse. My child's old enough to know who I am. I'm sure he loves me.

Emotionally, it turned me right off, to the point where I started drinking heavily, getting into drugs, I wouldn't go in to work, I wouldn't sleep. I was trying to fill up that hole of emptiness that was there. Emotionally, I was unstable. Physically, I was unstable because I wasn't taking care of myself. Mentally, I was definitely unstable. My outlook on life—there was none. I didn't know what I was doing wrong or what I was supposed to do. I felt lost, because this is the child my parents didn't want me to have and now my mother has taken him from me, and emotionally I was just confused. I didn't think it was fair.

My cousin, we've been the best of friends. One day she said to me, she actually grabbed me by the back of my head and said, "Look, you can't change the past, but it's not going to do you any good to go on the way you have." She explained to me that my mother's old. "There's going to be a day when your mother won't be able to take care of him and you're going to get him back." Every day when I wake up, I strive to get him back. Everything I do is to get him back. If I see a pair of baby shoes or a sweater, I'll buy it, I'll put it aside for him. I work towards getting him back.

Mentally, I think I'm more stable than I've been in my whole entire life. Physically, I'm very healthy, I take care of myself. And emotionally, because of my cousin and a lot of other people, I've been able to regain what I once had. What I do now is just try and work towards getting him back, and that's probably the biggest dream I've ever had. People have dreams: they want to be doctors, nurses, athletes and whatever. I work towards getting him back. He was my life.

I wasn't taught right from wrong. My parents are more corrupt than I am, actually. I have a very weird tale about my birth. My older sister is my mother. She had me a year and a half after her first child. I thought he was my nephew, but actually he's my brother. She could not handle having two, so she gave me to her mother. When I was five years old, the adoption papers were signed. So my mother and father are actually my grandparents, and I think that has the biggest twist ever. I only found out when I was eighteen. I went hysterical. I actually did freak out.

From kindergarten to Grade 7 everything was fine. Once I hit Grade 8, I don't know what happened. I fell into the wrong crowd. I wanted to be like everyone else. My mother was very strict. She forbid me to do just about anything that was fun. My mother was abusive. Her way of disciplining was to knock you out. There's never been anything extreme that I've done, that I can remember, but I can remember getting hit for it. My parents used things like extension cords, belt buckles, venetian blind cords, shoes, metal spoons. I just started getting ruthless and reckless, and did I ever get into trouble for it.

I think from birth we didn't like each other. She never really considered me as her child. I don't believe that I was ever accepted. It's something I've always thought—the attitude that I didn't really belong—and when I found that I wasn't even a part of that family, it kind of clicked. My family are professional liars. They're great at covering things up. I try not to dwell on it. I guess I'm in denial: "Oh, it's no big deal, who cares?" And I just leave it at that.

What hurts is not really knowing who my real father is. My sister won't tell me. She thinks that I don't need to know and I think that's why we don't talk. It's affected my life in such a big way that I want to know. Because of the fact that I've lost my son, I don't talk to my mother and I don't talk to my sister. I don't really talk to many people. I feel like I can't trust everybody else. You're lied to and then your child is stolen away from you. To me, it seems like there's this really big plan, this big plot. I really believe that they want to see me fail.

I am now a manager with the same company that I was with before. It's a retail company. I run fifteen different stores. It's fun. I work hard and save. I put it away. I have my own apartment. And I'm alive! It's easier now than it was before, when I first lost him. Now I enjoy life. Maybe if my family would come and visit me...but I take that in stride. When I'm ready, I'm going to go back into the courts and say, "I want my child back. Look, I've got this, I've done this, I've done that. I want my child back. I deserve to have my child back. He deserves to be with me. Nobody knows him better. Nobody can raise him better."

I think I'm waiting till I'm done being a kid. Everyone thinks of me as an adult, and in some aspects I am. I've got money and I'm stable, but I'm not done being a kid. That's what I'm waiting for. We go from child to adult. There's nothing in between. It'll happen. I think it might even happen this year. When I'm ready I'll know.

■

I'm doing this interview because I know I'm not the only teen mom out there. There are a lot of girls out there who feel lost. And there are a lot of teen mothers out there who've lost their children and are in that rut that I was in, and they can't seem to find their way out. I sympathize with them. Emotionally, I can feel their pain. It feels like the world is coming down on them.

I also know how hard it is to take care of a child. I'm doing this to show people that it's not the end of the world and there is a way out. There is a light at the end of the tunnel. The way I see it, keep strong and work towards a goal. If you make a goal and you work towards that goal, you feel a lot better when you get there. Everyone has the ability to do everything they want. I'm not telling teenagers to go out and have kids, because that would be wrong. I know how difficult it is. If you have one, your whole life is supposed to change. There's no more parties, no more guys, no more hanging out with the friends. All that changes because you have a child. That child has to go everywhere you go. You have to concentrate mostly on that child. To those teenagers who want kids, I tell them, sit back and think about it, because it's tough. Why take away youth? There's plenty of time. There's no reason to jump into it and have them right now. If you're financially stable, if you've got the money to do it, then by all means, but most people aren't. Actually, 99.9 percent of us aren't.

Teenagers that actually have kids at this point, all I can say is: Keep your head up, keep trying. Keep working hard at it, because it all pays off. It really does, when your child turns around and says, "I love you, Mom." When your child is sixteen or seventeen, the age we are now, you can sit down with your child and talk to them. Stop the cycle that's been going on for the longest time: teenagers having children. The way I see it, it's up to our generation to stop that cycle. More and more every day you hear about ten- and twelve-year-olds having kids, and that's ridiculous. For a sixteen-year-old to have a child—it's ridiculous. I think it's up to our generation to stop it. We have the biggest weapon right now, and that's our kids. If we can raise our children and teach them right from wrong from the very start, then the world will be a better place.

Anastasia

tells her

Basically, if you don't have anyone, you're on your own. That was my case. My family knew about the abortion. They always gave me grief after that. That was part of the reason I left Belgium. I was five months pregnant at that time. I had no money, nowhere to go. My family wouldn't support me, I was still at school. There was no way I was going to have a baby and give it a life of welfare. I thought, it's the best thing to do, but I was scared to death. My sister begged my boyfriend at that time to at least go with me for the abortion. He didn't want to.

That first pregnancy, I wanted to have the baby. My boyfriend and I agreed on that. Then he turned out to be some kind of weirdo and he dumped me and I had to go through the whole abortion thing alone, which was hell. I was nineteen when it happened. For three months after that I had to be hospitalized, because I wasn't eating, I wasn't drinking, I was like a zombie. I thought, I'm never hav-

Anastasia wanted to tell me everything, including the lies she had told to the adoption agency. She needed to be sure that I understood why she had to let someone else raise her baby.

ing another abortion. I would never be able to handle it, I'll go wacko.

I moved to Australia and got a job in an advertising agency. About a year and a half later, I met this guy who was from Canada. Edward was gorgeous and really nice. I found out that he was married, but going for a divorce. We had a week altogether. Everywhere he travelled, he kept calling me. He really cared about me. He even cried when he was leaving. I thought, he'll never call me. I felt bad, but life goes on.

But he did call. He would talk to me for about two hours and it was the same as when he was in Australia. Then he wanted to send me a ticket to come and visit him here. I was flattered. I thought, a guy doesn't fly you across the world just to have sex with you and dump you. So I was really happy about it and I accepted.

Before I left, I found out about being an au pair girl, a nanny. It turned out that there was this job in Montreal, Canada, with a French Canadian family living in Brussels at the time. I told Edward. I said, "How about if I took this job and went to Canada for a year?" He said, "Great." I thought this was going so well, he wants me there.

I came here a month after the family moved here. Edward came to pick me up at the airport. He had a rose and I thought, this is as romantic as anybody can get. Everything worked perfectly for a couple of months. We were sleeping together. He used condoms—I asked him to—and I was on the pill. I thought that protection shouldn't only be his thing to do. Also, it would be safer to have two methods at a time.

He took me out to meet his parents. His divorce was coming. I thought, this was serious. Over Christmas, we went to visit a friend of mine in New Orleans. We had stopped using condoms because neither of us had a disease. But when we went to New Orleans, I left my pills at home. I thought when I got back I could take them for two days to make up, but it didn't work.

In New Orleans, we started to argue. He would give me shit for nothing. We came back and everything was going down really fast. He dumped me.

In January, I had my period. I thought, great, I'm saved. But then I didn't get it in March. I took one of those pregnancy tests in the drugstore and it was positive. I went to a doctor and I was panicked. I said, "How can this be?" He said, "It wasn't your period, it's just bleeding that you can have in your first month of being pregnant." By that time three months had passed and there was no way I could have an abortion, which was good because I didn't want one anyway.

I was thinking, what should I do? Should I tell Edward? Should I keep the child and let him know? But I don't want any of my kids to be juggling between me and the father. Who's going to have child custody? But I didn't want to have a child with this guy. I knew he wouldn't want me to have an abortion. He would force himself to take responsibility, but he wouldn't want it. I didn't want to fight with him to see whether or not he's going to pay child support. I didn't want a child to have the feeling that he or she wasn't wanted. I wasn't ready to be a mother. I had plans. I was only twenty-one years old.

I was working here as an au pair, not making much money. I was taking care of three children. Children need diapers, clothes, entertainment, medical care. I don't have anything for myself, how am I going to provide for a child? If I have nothing to eat for a day, I can make it, but not for a baby. I can't be that selfish. At the end, I was trying to be as selfless as possible, by making the right decision for the baby first. I had no medical coverage. I didn't go to the doctor till I was seven months pregnant, I couldn't afford it. There were no people that I knew well enough to ask for help. I didn't tell the people I worked for till I was seven months pregnant. I wasn't showing at all. All this time I was careful: I took no medication, didn't drink or anything.

I thought about adoption. But how am I going to handle adoption? I thought, well, I'm on my own. I looked in the phone book for Adoption Services, but what do I look for? How do I know I'm getting the best service? How do I know the baby will be placed with the right people? I called the child protection society and spoke to a man, Bernard. I said I wanted to place a baby for adoption. I wanted some information about how it works. He asked me how far along I was and if I had a doctor. When he heard I didn't have a doctor, he asked me to come see him.

The meeting was not scary. It was very private; I liked that. He was nice. I knew it was going to work. He asked me why I wanted to place the baby for adoption. I said, "The father's not around and that's the choice that I made." So he explained to me how it works. He said the birth parents get to choose the adoptive parents if that's what they want to do. He asked me about my medical history, what my family was like, as well as information about the father and his family— the type of information needed so that the adoptive parents could know more about the kid when it grew up. The only thing I lied about was the birth father. I told him that he was a one-night stand in New York. I did that because Bernard told me that, if they have the birth father's name, they would have to track him down to get him to sign the consent forms. Bernard accepted the story. He asked me to tell him the kind of people I want, if there was anything that I wanted them to be like. "What kind of life do you want your child to have with these people?"

I said, "I don't want the kind of couple that stays home on the weekend; dad is mowing the grass and mom is making cookies. I want people who have a life. I want them to be open-minded, understanding. I want them to be very young, mentally. My baby deserves the best." In this case, I had the opportunity to pick what I thought would be the best. So I was very happy, because I was going to make the first import-ant decision in my baby's life, which was who she/he was going to live with and what his/her life was going to be like.

Bernard kept looking, and he couldn't find anybody for about two months. By then I was eight months pregnant. Then he said, "I have this one couple, Paula and Michael. I think they might be the people you're looking for." I was in the office when he called them. He said, "I have this birth mother who wants to know more about you." So they gave him a huge envelope of pictures. Everybody thought they were a perfect match. I wanted to meet them. I wanted to go with my gut feeling, so I talked to them. I wanted to know what kind of life they had. I asked what they did every weekend. I said, "What if the baby turns out very sick?" They said, "There's no problem. We would be able to support the child financially. We would be there." I said, "I don't know if it's a boy or a girl, does it matter to you?" They said, "No, we would like to know to be able to do the shopping, but it doesn't matter." I said, "Life nowadays is different, and what if my child turns out to be gay? Or has different preferences? How would you react to that?" They said, "We are very open about that. We have friends who are gay. We're open, we understand. We don't see it as weird. It makes no difference to us. There's no way we'll ever turn our back on our child."

I thought they were perfect. I went mostly on the gut feeling I had when I saw them. I loved them. I wanted to say, "Will you adopt me too?" They were exactly what I wanted. There was so much similarity between her and I, it was scary. And the best part was that they had spent nine years in Belgium, they spoke French. They were perfect.

I told them that I couldn't afford to see a doctor. I told them, "I want you to know I did my best. I ate healthy, I didn't take any medication. I didn't go wacko and go rollerblading or anything like that. I don't smoke, I didn't drink and I don't do drugs." After they left, Bernard said, "They said you were a doll." I told him I really liked them. So I went with them. When he told them that I chose them, they were going crazy because they were so happy.

Now I knew my medical costs would be covered, I went to the doctor once a week. The people I worked for made me understand that I had to go. I had nowhere to go, and Bernard found me a women's shelter that helps pregnant girls.

I read that, at this stage of the pregnancy, the baby can hear you and recognize your voice. I tried to sing a kid's song, knowing that she didn't understand anything. Sometimes I would be by myself and I would be talking, and I'm sure people looked at me like I was a psycho. She would kick like crazy before I would go to bed, to the point that she would really hurt me. So I thought that, maybe if I rock myself, it would calm her down. I had this rocking-chair that I ordered from the States because I heard that babies would be rocked even though they're inside. Then I would go to bed and it would be fine. It's funny, that little person could decide, "I want this, I want that."

You feel really beautiful, you feel perfect. Your hands and feet are swollen and your whole body is huge, but you feel perfect. You're the most beautiful woman on earth. I really missed it after she came out.

When I began to have contractions, the staff of the house drove me to the hospital. The contractions were like the worst thing that can happen to you. I was in pain like you can't imagine. I had some woman from the house as the labour coach, but it was her first time, so she didn't know what to say or do. I felt again like I was by myself. I had to beg for drugs. They gave me small injections. I slept about half an hour the whole night.

I had called Bernard the night before and asked him if Paula and Michael would like to be at the hospital the day the baby would be born. Paula came and was outside in a waiting-room. Michael was away on a business trip, but he was jumping on the first plane. She wasn't in the room with me when the baby was born. I wanted it to be my own thing, mine and my baby's and no one else's. They were going to have her for the rest of her life, so I wanted that at least.

When she was born, it was very easy. I felt nothing, she slipped through in a matter of seconds. The doctor told me it was very simple, very fast. I didn't need any stitches. It was perfect. All the time I was pregnant I worried that I was so small, and she turned out to be the biggest baby in the nursery. The nurse asked me, "Do you want the adopting mother to come in right now?" I said, "No, I want a few minutes with my baby by myself." It was weird, because she was screaming her head off and when they gave her to me, she stopped, just like that. I thought, wow, I have this power over her, it's amazing.

It felt weird, though. Some people have this motherly feeling, this love, right away. I remember kissing her, because I have to kiss her; it's my baby, at least do that, because she would feel rejected or something like that. It was like kissing a stranger. She was staring at me. You know they say that babies can't see. Well, she could see. I would move my head around and she would follow me with her eyes. She was looking at me and it felt uncomfortable. I said, "Nurse, come and get the baby." I was in the twilight zone, really tired.

Paula came in. She made it a point not to get too close, which I appreciated. She totally respected me being there and holding my own child. She waited until I asked her if she wanted to hold her. She said, "Oh, she's so cute," just about what anybody who has a baby would say. She took her in her arms and she went to sit down in a rocking-chair. The doctor and everybody was coming to check how I was. I was answering, but not really listening. I was looking at her in the rocking-chair and thinking, "This is it, it's over. It's not my baby any more." Then the feelings about the baby I didn't have when I was pregnant and when she was in my arms suddenly all hit me in the face. From the moment I felt it was over, I lost her, it hit me that this was everything I've always wanted. She was in my body, but now there's nothing. I panicked. There was something inside of me saying, "Just take the baby and go." These were things I didn't know I would feel.

I was so tired, I didn't have the energy to say anything. Somehow I was relieved that the whole pregnancy thing was over. Something had just finished and something was starting. Paula stayed there for what seemed an eternity, holding her, to the point where I felt frustrated: "OK, give her back."

She probably stayed there ten minutes; to me it was like half an hour. Then she gave her back to me and said she was going to let me rest.

Bernard called me twenty minutes after she was born. He asked me how I was doing, and he said congratulations. I felt, congratulations for what? What's the difference, I'm losing her anyway? Then I slept for about two hours.

I woke up and went to the nursery to see her. I held her. She was so tiny, it was scary. I unwrapped her and counted her fingers and toes—I guess every mother on earth does that—checked her ears, the shape of the head. She's normal, she looks normal. After I left the hospital, I remembered her smell. I don't know if it was on me, but I could smell it for a week or so.

Michael had just arrived from the airport, so I was sitting there with them. They didn't know what to say to me. Paula kissed me and hugged me, asked how I was. There were all these babies, and they were looking and they didn't know which one it was. It was kind of funny. They all look the same, all wrinkled. They found her and they held her. I was leaving. I mean, I couldn't walk, my butt was hurting me, my stomach was in pain. They saw I was leaving, so they came over and thanked me and hugged me.

When I woke up in the morning, the nurses asked me, "Do you want to stay here a couple more days?" So I thought, I'd have a couple more days with her and I could get attached to her really close; or I go right now and I don't get attached to her, which would probably be better for me, because if I bond too much then it's over, I'll go nuts. I said, "No, she's going the same time as me, but with them."

I got dressed. I went to see her. The doctor was there, checking her. And she was screaming. He said, "Do you want to hold her?" And I said, "Sure." I held her, and she stopped right away from screaming. It was weird. And I felt really uncomfortable. I felt like I had some kind of magical power or something. I never knew that a mother had such a power on her child, that a child can recognize you just by smelling you, just by knowing that it's you and no one else. I talked a little bit to her, trying to explain why I had to do it, that she was going to be OK, that they were really nice people. I said goodbye. I was thinking, "I must be completely nuts talking to a baby who doesn't understand anything," but I had to do it. I can't just leave and not let her know anything. I knew I wasn't going to be able to handle having them take her away. I left her and I took off.

It was hell. It was really hard. At that point I felt like I had lost the baby, like she was dead. I took a cab back to the group home. I was in really bad shape. I remember seeing this baby on the street and I started crying. It was like that for about a month: I would see a child and start crying. I went to see Bernard. He was sure that I had chosen the right people for my child. He said that I should be happy to know that she was going to get everything that I wanted her to have but unfortunately couldn't give her myself. I didn't sleep for about a week. I didn't have a life. I would cry the whole night and sleep the whole day. I would do nothing. People said, "You know you shouldn't be doing this, it's not good for you. You have to let go." I would get really upset when people would tell me to let go.

A couple of weeks later I went to see Bernard to sign some papers. I was going through the twenty-five days of the possibility of changing my mind if I wanted to. It crossed my mind several times, mostly in the last days, but I didn't change my mind. I was more realistic at that point than before she was born, because I'd seen her. She was a human being, a little person. I asked Bernard if I could talk to the parents. It's not allowed, I'm not supposed to have any contact with them. But Bernard understood. That's what I really appreciate about him: he has feelings. He's not only doing his job, he also knows that it's hard. I needed the person who was taking care of my baby to tell me herself how things were going.

Paula was really nervous. I guess it was from the fear of me changing my mind. I figured, she's nervous because she's afraid to lose her, and she's afraid because this baby really means something to her. So I thought, "This is perfect. This is good." But it was hard. She asked me how I was and I cried. She didn't know what to say. She said, "She's really doing fine." There was nothing else I wanted to know except that she was doing fine. Bernard said, "Why don't we just wait until the twenty-five days are over. Nobody's ever a hundred percent sure." I looked at him and said, "I am. I'm a hundred percent sure. I'm not going to change my mind."

The twenty-five days were over. I felt kind of relieved that it was over, there was no more choice. I was glad that it was forcing me, telling me, "This is finished, you have to move on." It was like one burden less on my shoulders. Up to that day, I had to make all these choices. I had to decide between abortion, adoption, motherhood. The whole thing was about choices. Finally there were no more choices to make.

I wanted to call them a second time to find out how she was. The first time was so close to the birth, so they were ecstatic and everything. Let's see how they're feeling now that they haven't slept for two months. Bernard called again. Paula said, "Everybody's fine. We are tired, but the happiness we feel inside is way stronger than needing the sleep. Every minute that we spend with her is wonderful." So that was good. I thought, "Now I have to stop bothering them. Now she's their baby. It's their family, their life. I'm not a part of it, I made the choice not to be a part of it. So I have to leave them alone." Which I didn't. I kept bugging them. They were sick of me after a while. I had those mother worries. Every mother worries about their child. I even went to the library to see when the baby should have vaccinations and stuff. I would say to Bernard, "It's been two months, has she had her vaccines, her checkup?" He's like, "Yeah, they're doing it. She's fine. She doesn't have any problems. She's really healthy. She has in her eyes a little sparkle. You look in her eyes and all you can see is happiness." She was going to people and smiling at everybody. They sent me pictures and videotapes. In the first year, every three months, you get pictures and letters from the adoptive parents. After that it's once a year, until she's eighteen. I asked for the videotape. I wanted to be able to hear her, to see her laughing and playing. The first year I actually had three videotapes.

It was hard. You're supposed to move on; but it's always there. Then at some point I thought, "Maybe this videotape thing isn't good for me. You hear them call each other 'Mom' and 'Dad.' I'm her mom." What was really hard was that they taped Mother's Day. And I thought, I didn't get Mother's Day and I'm her mother. I found it really cruel to tape Mother's Day.

I was seeing a social worker, trying to get some help to accept that it is the way it is, and that I should move on. I had thought of suicide, it had gotten to the point where I thought of killing myself. I thought I was a monster. I did the worst thing a mother could do and I couldn't live with it. She really helped me. I had nobody to listen to me at that point. My family didn't know, I had nobody here, she was the only one I could talk to. Getting help was the best thing to do.

Ten months later, I called Bernard. He told me that Michael had a job offer in Belgium. Paula had asked how I would feel about it. I knew they were not going to base their decision on what I think, but I still appreciated that they didn't just take off. It hasn't been a year yet and they're going to take her away. I'm planning to stay here to be near her, and they're moving. Then I thought about it rationally and I took it as a sign that I'm not letting go like I should. This is a way to tell me it's time to let go. They moved to Belgium. It wasn't as hard as I thought it would be. They promised to keep in touch. I felt the cord was finally cut: she was gone, she wasn't even in the same country. It felt like a loss again, a second one. I think I went back into a light depression.

They sent Bernard some gifts for me. I cried, it really touched me. Every time something like that would happen, I would love them more. But her birthday passed and nothing from them. I started getting mad, 'cause I was supposed to get something around her birthday, like pictures or letters. I had given them a baby book that I wanted them to fill for me through the years—first teeth, first steps and stuff like that. I was not getting anything, and I freaked out.

I remember my counsellor told me that I should go and get her something. I felt, "What for? They're giving her everything. What's the use? It's going to be cheap." I felt it was a kind of competition. She said, "You have to do it. No matter what you get, if it's a card or a letter, they will keep it for her to have later. She will know that you didn't forget about her." I thought about that, and she was right. So I went to get her a card and a book. I gave it to Bernard to send. I feel completely positive about the whole thing. The parents gave me more than I expected. They always respected me and my feelings. They make me part of her life, they make sure that she knows about me. When I send something to her, they don't put it away in the closet. If I send a stuffed animal, they let her play with it. I send her clothes and they put them on her. It's like I have this connection with my daughter. It's strange, hard to explain, it's a gut feeling inside of me. If she wouldn't be happy, I would know it and I wouldn't be able to go on the way I am right now. I do believe that all mothers and their children have that kind of contact.

That's how I feel, and I'm happy about the whole thing. It's the most mature, responsible and rational decision that I've made in my life. At one point my counsellor told me that I "gave her up." I don't like that term. I didn't leave her on the steps of the police station or the hospital. I'm still checking on how she's doing. I don't call it "giving up," I call it "placing for adoption." Bernard had said, "You've placed her for adoption, because you wanted her to have the best. She's getting the best now." What more could I want? She's happy. She has everything she needs. I don't provide the happiness and the health, but she has it. Now, whether I am happy or sad, I find it irrelevant. It's not the purpose of the whole adoption thing.

I'm sad that I don't see her—the first steps, the first tooth. I'm missing everything, missing her discovering life. I love her, I love her to death. If tomorrow they were to call Bernard and say there's a problem, we need a heart, we need something, I'm there. I wouldn't even think twice about it. If that means I have to give my life for her, I'll do it. Now I'm crying.

I always did everything for myself, to the point where I thought, I'm the most selfish person on earth. I found myself selfish for leaving my family. I didn't take their feelings into consideration. I was a total bitch to my mother. Having a baby changes you completely. I found that I'm not like I thought I was. I'm not selfish. If I was selfish, I would have kept her with me. You let go because you know that is what is best for them, it's what they need.

I'm working as a nanny now. I find I'm very much attracted by family law. I want to deal with what has to do with divorces and adoptions, but always working with kids. Working as a nanny is allowing me to stay here, get landing papers, go on with my life, go to school, get my life together, make my dreams come true. I have a boyfriend, I met him six months ago. He's really supportive. He knows about the baby. When I met him, I wanted him to know there's more in my life than our relationship. He accepted it.

I didn't tell her father. I keep track of where he is. The

reason I'm keeping track of him is not to hunt him down. I have a feeling—I hope that one day my daughter will come back and will want to meet me. I want to be able to tell her where her father lives. I don't care what he thinks, what he feels. There's no one else on earth that matters to me except her. I guess there'll always be this love, because he's the father of my child and he did mean a lot to me. I have to live with the fact that I didn't tell him that he had a child, that I had to lie. I really hope that everything is going to turn out great, 'cause if not, I'll never be able to live with myself.

I bought many books about adoption and read them. I wanted to understand what adoptees go through and what other birth mothers and adoptive parents go through. Paula and Michael are not selfish people, but they're going to be selfish because they're going to think, "We raised her, we gave her everything." Which is understandable. They'll be jealous if she wants to see me and they'll be hurt, but they will always support her. If one day she says she wants to meet me, I'm sure they'll be one hundred percent behind her. Twenty years from now, I want to be able to see my daughter if she wants to see me. I'm curious, I want to know what she looks like. I want her to know who she is and where she's from and what I was like. People might think I'm pathetic, that I'm hanging on to everything. If she doesn't want to see me, then that's all right too. But she'll know that I remembered her birthdays—not that I placed her for adoption and went away and didn't care. From what I read, it's important for the child to know that I cared and wanted to know about her. I don't want to be a stranger. I want to be part of her life. I intend to work really hard on that.

Chloe

 *tells her* **STORY**

I'm due in two weeks. I'm in a state of constant uncomfortable. I'm nineteen years old. I left home when I was fourteen, my first year of high school. I first got pregnant when I was fourteen and had the baby when I was fifteen. I was pretty screwed up then, so I was in a detention centre. I didn't realize I was pregnant until I was five and a half months pregnant, so there was very little time for any decisions to be made. It was too late for me to have an abortion. I've been on the street ever since I was fourteen, off and on. I have my own apartment now. I've had my own place for the past year.

I don't know why I left home, now, when I think about it. I had everything. My mother was a little bit overbearing; that's the only reason I left home. She was just so clingy to me that I couldn't take it any more. She wasn't letting me grow up and go out, or have friends or anything. So I just left. I wasn't abused, mentally, physically or anything. Just too many rules.

My mom was just so...I was everything my mother had. I was

Chloe is nine months pregnant. Through her tears and with a sense of humour, she told me about the baby she placed for adoption when she was fifteen, her life on the street, and the hopes she has for her unborn child.

my mom's reason for living. She'd go to work so she could put food on the table for me. She'd come home, sit with me, she never had any other friends. It was just her and her daughter. I couldn't go out 'cause my mom would get lonely. She didn't have any friends. My dad left when I was a kid. He's not a very nice person. I grew up in the Midwest. We moved here to Los Angeles when I was almost twelve. When my mom got here, she couldn't make any friends.

The day I left home, I got up at eight o'clock on a Saturday morning. I had started hanging around downtown, knowing a couple of people. I had to meet this guy Winston at noon. He was seventeen, but he thought I was eighteen. I got up and I was showering and I was just hyped because I was going to meet this cute guy. My mom was in a bad mood, and she came and threw the bathroom door open and said, "If you leave, don't bother coming back to get your stuff." I guess she wanted me to stay at home with her. So I said, "Fine," and just left. I was stupid. One of the biggest regrets of my life was leaving home. It became a regret when I smartened up—I guess, sixteen or seventeen years old. I started thinking, that was really stupid. I hurt my mother, hurt myself. Now, when I think about it, there was absolutely no reason.

Winston was a street person, so it wasn't very hard to hang out with people. I hung out with everybody who lived on the streets, for about two months. My mom used to dress up like a man and sit in the donut place on the corner and watch me and make sure that nothing happened to me. One night, it was about eleven or twelve at night, there was a bunch of us walking up the street and my mother grabbed hold of a police officer and said, "See that young girl over there? She's my daughter. She's got a Missing Persons Report out on her and you guys aren't looking for her and I'm sick of being the one following her around, so could you please take her into custody." They took me into custody and I signed myself into a government group home.

Finally I did go back with my mom, but I left again. Then they put me in another group home. There were a lot of problems with that. I ran away again and got a title slapped on me: Habitual Runaway. So the next time they put me in a place that's one of the most "closed custody" group homes that you can get. They say it's for kids who are illegal prostitutes. I wasn't a prostitute. The government youth worker, she hated me. She didn't have any children of her own, so she had this book that she followed which was supposed to be on basic behaviour of kids. I didn't follow the book, so she hated me and she stuck me in this group home, this closed custody...jail.

That's when I found I was pregnant. I didn't know, I didn't miss any periods. I was throwing up a lot, we couldn't figure out why. Every time I went to see a doctor, they'd say, "There's nothing wrong with your stomach or your lungs," 'cause every time, at a meal, if I'd fill myself too full, I'd cough and then I'd throw up. They kept saying, "There's nothing wrong." So my mother got me on a day pass and we went and saw my family doctor. During the physical, she asked me about my periods, when the last time I had sex was. I told her four, five months ago. She told me I was pregnant and that there wasn't much time for me to make any decisions: whether to have a safe abortion, put it up for adoption or keep it. I was too young to keep it. I knew I was. I couldn't take care of myself. I couldn't live with my mother. I couldn't live on my own. I couldn't be in a closed custody group home with a baby. And I knew I wasn't mentally stable enough for a child.

Before I knew I was pregnant, I was pretty heavily involved in drugs and alcohol, staying up for days on end. Sleep deprivation was a big thing; I'd get a kick out of it. Being awake for three or four days on acid, then the next few days sober but still hallucinating 'cause I hadn't slept in so long. So it was like I was still on drugs. Sometimes I'd go a week without sleeping. Then I'd sleep for three days, wake up and do it all over again.

I was panhandling. The way I remember it, it wasn't hard at all. It was fun. I could do whatever I wanted. It was really easy to get money. I didn't have to do anything morally wrong or anything against my values. It was more fun for me to be on the streets than to be at home.

I don't know how the baby survived, to be completely honest. To be as healthy as it was, I don't know how it happened, because I was seriously into LSD. I never did hard drugs. I was never into cocaine or heroin, but I was into LSD.

Big-time LSD, PCP. I used to sleep all over—shelters, places that were abandoned. I never had to sleep outdoors. I always had some form of shelter. People would buy pizza and bring it down to the kids at the shelter. They'd just drop inside and say, "Here." I lived on pizza slices and day-old donuts for a year. For the last month and a half of my pregnancy, I lived in a group home. They fed me really good. I packed on the weight.

Winston didn't know I was pregnant, because he left me before he even found out. I had heard he went to San Francisco. Me and a friend tried to hitchhike there, to look for him. I never found him until two and a half years later. I had a picture of the baby to show Winston when I ran back into him. It was a really big soap opera. He left his wife for me, then he left me, then he tried to come back to me. Winston was being a complete idiot. But he was, like, my first love. I'm just crying because I remember him and the baby.

The people that adopted the baby were really nice. I got to meet with three couples, and that one couple was really nice. They were the people that I picked to be the "adoptees." My doctor, two lawyers, myself and the adoptees were the only people involved. That was it. They didn't pay me for it or anything. They paid the hospital bill. I didn't stay in the hospital overnight. I stayed in fourteen hours after the baby was born, and then I left and went back to the group home. I never actually saw them while I was in the hospital. I imagine that they were there, because they were phoned and told that I was in labour. My doctor was there and a woman from the group home, and me—that was it. It was pretty hard. Nobody was very supportive. Everything was really cold. Nobody was very caring about what I was going through. The doctors didn't even let me hold the baby. They didn't want to tell me anything, if he was OK—they were just really cold. They were just like I was a machine, a producer of a product. I don't think I'd ever want to do it again, give a baby up for adoption.

They let me name him, but I don't know the couple's last name. I named the baby Winston, and as far as I know they kept the name. There's no agreement that they have to tell him he's adopted, but they said that if I wrote a letter they would give it to him when he's sixteen years old, or if he ever asks if he's adopted or whatever. They said they'd give it to him and my name, in case he ever wants to track me down. I don't know if I would do it if I adopted a baby. It would probably be one of the hardest things to do, to say, "This is your real mother. Go find her." But they said that they would.

The couple sent me pictures up until the second Christmas afterward. I thought it was really great for the first little while, because these people sent me pictures of the baby, and then they just kind of stopped. I got two pictures, and they never sent me any more. I wonder what he looks like. It's just really hard for me.

They sent me letters. They don't have to keep any kind of contact with me at all. There was no agreement that they had to write and tell me that everything was OK or keep in contact with me or anything. It was just something, I guess, they did out of their heart. I kind of appreciate that they did, kind of wish they hadn't. It was kind of like rubbing your face in shit. That's the way it feels to me now. It just seems kind of cruel, to send pictures of somebody's child when they don't have custody of their child. At the time it didn't, but now it seems really cruel. I'm sorry for crying now.

I think about him on his birthday and on Mother's Day. For the rest of the year, I try not to think about it, but that's very hard. I cry when I think about it. It didn't really hit me until one and a half years later. It hit me pretty hard, on Mother's Day. I started crying for no reason. All my friends didn't understand, they just thought I was having some bad trip or something. When I see someone walking down the street with a stroller, a young girl with a brand-new baby, I think, "Well, I could've done that." Then I think, "No, I couldn't have." It was best. I did the right thing. I know I did the right thing, I still know I did the right thing, but it's pretty hard to accept.

I know that he's doing a lot better than I could've ever given him. They can give him ten times more than I ever could. They've got money. I could've never given him a house. I probably couldn't have afforded to send him to a community college. He's doing a lot better. I don't even know if I want him to find me one day. I don't know how I'd handle it. It would really hurt.

My only goal, so far, is to graduate high school. Once that happens, I don't know where I'm going. Actually, I was in high school up until a month and a half ago. I've gone back every year since I left home, and I've dropped out every year. But I did complete Grade 9. It's just hard to go. When you live on the streets, you live a lot, you learn a lot. You learn stuff about what it takes to be able to survive in the world. So when you sit in a math class, they tell you that $A + B \times C = M$, you think, "What the hell do I need to know this for? This isn't going to get me anywhere." Things just don't make sense. I think I've learned more in the five years I've been on the street than I ever could during high school—life skills, living skills. I shouldn't have any problems surviving in society, except that everything makes me so angry because it's so stupid. High school is so stupid. Algebra and stuff like that has never seemed to come in handy since I left high school. So I don't understand why I should have to learn it. I think the important subjects are reading, science and art. I don't think there should be school past Grade 6. I think you should learn everything you need to know by Grade 6.

Now I'm eight and a half months pregnant. I've been a lot luckier in this relationship. I've been with the father—well, I refer to him as the father—for a year and a half. We broke up for a month or so, and it just so happened that I got pregnant somewhere between before we broke up and when we got back together. All the medical stuff points to the father being my common-law husband, Max. He doesn't really care who the father is, he just wants to know. He says he'll be there. He says it's hard for him to say what's going to happen, but as far as he thinks, even if he's not the father, he'll still consider the child his. But like he says, it's easy to say that now, but it's really hard for him to tell what's actually going to happen.

The pregnancy was a complete accident. It was all because I bought five litres of cranberry juice. We never used protection. We used protection when we were first together, until we got all our tests done and realized there was no reason to be using protection except for pregnancy. And the pregnancy never happened. All of a sudden it did. They say cranberry juice cleans out your system. With men, it can clean out their system and really increase their sperm count. I bought five litres and got pregnant shortly afterwards.

I decided to keep it, because I don't really believe in

abortion. I don't think I could go through that. I'm against abortion for myself, not for other people. I'm not one of those people that get outside abortion clinics to protest. It's what's in your best interest. If it's best, then go for it. It's not in my best interest. There's so many people out there that want children, that can't have children, why not give them the chance instead of having an abortion? I read in the paper that there was over two million abortions performed last year in the United States, and that's just the ones they could keep track of. There could be ten million women running around who can't have children, who are just waiting for children to adopt so they can make their life everything it's supposed to be. They're still childless, and there's two million dead babies. If it's something that someone wants to do, I don't put them down for it—but it's life. The heart starts beating at four to six weeks, or something like that. People can have abortions up to three months. At three months it's got fingers and toes. I don't know how people can go through with it with a clear conscience.

Back then, I couldn't have been a proper parent, I was too young. Maybe not physically too young to be a parent, but I was definitely mentally too young. I'm hoping now—I'm going to give it the best shot that I can. I think that with enough support I can do it. My mother and me are on really good terms now, she's really supportive of me. She wasn't, but she is now. I have a pretty good group of friends that have already had children. If I need help, I can just call whoever and they'll come. Max does everything for me. Totally. Massages me, massages my feet, takes my boots off, helps me roll over on to my side. Without all this support, I don't think that I could do it.

Now I'm on welfare. I was doing better panhandling than I am on welfare. I'll panhandle two or three days out of the month, fairly close to the end of the month.

I'm kind of scared to be a mom. I'm not really happy, I'm not angry, I'm not sad. Getting a little bit anxious, but not really scared. I have a dog. She's really well behaved. I look at my dog and think, if I can do as good a job with my kid as I do with my dog, then I'm doing OK, because I have one of the best dogs in the world. She listens to everything I say. I know it sounds rude comparing a dog to a child, but when you think about it, the first couple of years are like a dog anyway. I think now that I've mastered the dog, I can move on to a child.

■

My advice to girls who will read this book is: if you're not ready to raise a child, let somebody else do it. I try not to preach anti-abortion, but there's so many women out there who can't have children. So if you're not ready for it, why not give somebody who is ready the chance? That's my advice. And good luck! I feel really sorry for people who are stuck in the situation and have to do something 'cause it's their only way. Like me. If I hadn't been so young, I wouldn't have done it. This baby is definitely going to be a lot more enjoyable. It's going to bring a lot more pleasure into my life than the last one, which is good.

Laura

tells her

I'm eighteen and a half. My boyfriend, Mike, is twenty-three. I met him a year ago, through my friend in my high school. We started being sexually active two months into the relationship. I don't know why, but I never got pregnant. We used condoms, but not all the time. Then I noticed I didn't get my period.

I did a pregnancy test and it was positive. So I went to a walk-in clinic that my friend referred me to. They did a urine test, and I was two months pregnant. I had made the decision to have an abortion even before I started having sex. I told the woman at the clinic that "This is what I want to do. I'm not having this kid. I'm too young, I can't support it. I don't want to bring it into the world when it's going to have a bad life."

I was living with Mike when I got pregnant. When I was

Though not yet old enough to legally buy cigarettes, Laura discussed how she has matured through moving out of her parents' house, living with her boyfriend and aborting her pregnancy.

sixteen, seventeen, and living at home, things were good, but I was having a hard time. I was in school, but I was doing drugs, mostly marijuana. My relationship with my parents got difficult. Mom would be overprotective of me. She wouldn't let me go out and I got really frustrated with that, not having my freedom.

I was over at Mike's place one night. He has a really cool apartment with a sauna and a pool, and I said, "My parents are really getting to me. I want to get away from them." That's when Mike asked me if I would move in with him, so I did. When I told my parents, they said, "There is nothing we can do. If you really want this, you're of a legal age to live by yourself." They offered to give me money lots of times.

Mike and I got along really good. We had fun with each other. We liked doing the same things. We were really compatible. He was really sweet. Most guys only want one thing, and after they get that one thing, which is sex, they don't want anything to do with you. He wasn't like that, he doesn't want to do that to me. He doesn't just want sex. There's more in our relationship, in life. Like the way you treat people, the way you have respect for somebody.

I didn't sleep with him for the first two months, because it was my first time and I wanted to wait. I wanted to see if he was the right person for me to make my commitment to. He was very polite and he treated me very good. I could tell he wasn't like other guys.

The first time we made love, he was hurting me. It was really painful for me and I was crying, and then he started to cry 'cause he didn't want to hurt me. I thought that was so sweet, because most guys can't let their emotions out. They are taught not to show feelings, to always be right, to remain cool. I thought it was cool that he could cry in front of me.

The first time with him, I pictured it being scary, because when I was twelve years old I was molested. It wasn't intercourse, it was penetration with fingers. It was scary for me. I knew this guy for a year before that happened. After that I thought sex would be scary. I did get counselling. I'm fine about it now. I just thought it would hurt really bad. It did hurt, but it wasn't that bad. Mike used a condom that first time. I got pregnant three months later.

During those three months, sometimes we didn't have any condoms. It would be on the spur of the moment and we would say, "OK, who cares?" The first time we didn't use a condom, Mike said, "I don't have any left. We'll get some more later. You won't get pregnant. Some of your girlfriends did it without and they didn't get pregnant. So we can do without." I felt a little uneasy about it. I said to him that I didn't want to put myself at risk in any way. He said, "Don't worry, we'll get some more later. We'll just do it this one time." I guess I was talked into it.

He said he got tested for AIDS or HIV. He said he got tested two months before we became sexually active. He said he used condoms with his other girlfriends most of the time, but not all the time. He had only slept with a couple of girls. I guess I believed him. I thought disease wouldn't happen.

Then he told me he didn't like using condoms because it pinched and hurt. So I said, "OK, you withdraw before you ejaculate." He did that a couple of times, but I don't think he did it every time—obviously not. I knew there were other methods, but I guess they seemed too unfamiliar to me—like IUDs. I don't want to stick something up there, a diaphragm or a sponge or foam. Then I decided to go on the pill. I was waiting to get my period so I could start the pill, and it never came.

I was panicking, because I thought for sure I was pregnant, because I know sometimes he would ejaculate in me.

When I told Mike, he said, "You're probably not. Just stop worrying about it." I had had a false alarm once before, so I said, "I think this time it's for real." It was very frustrating. I wanted him to be more supportive with me. After I was a week late, I thought I might as well make sure if I am or I'm not pregnant. So I went to a drugstore with my sister. There were so many different kinds of pregnancy tests, so I chose the one that was quickest. It was very expensive too. It was $14.99 for one. There was a sign at the counter that said if you want the pharmacist to do it for you, it was $10. But I didn't know how they would go about doing it, so I didn't feel comfortable doing it that way. I wanted to do it by myself. The instructions said it was 99.9 percent effective.

When I did the test, I was in my parents' house, visiting them. I went into the bathroom and did the test. Two blue lines if you were pregnant and one if you weren't. In a minute it was blue. Then I went into my sister's room and I told her. I threw the test in the garbage so my parents wouldn't find it. I wasn't surprised at the positive result, because I thought I was pregnant. I was thinking about the abortion, how much money it would be. I was a little bit depressed. I was thinking, "How could I be so irresponsible? How could I let this happen?" I didn't go to my mom. I don't know why I didn't. Maybe it was because they didn't approve of Mike. They still don't like him. They think I can do better.

I told Mike when he came to pick me up from my parents' house. I said, "It's true, I am pregnant." I said, "What am I going to do? How am I going to go about getting an abortion? How much is it?" Mike was supportive, but he was afraid for the same reasons that I was a little afraid. It was all new to me. It had never happened to me before. I didn't know if there would be any effects, if I could have kids later on. I don't want any now, but later, when I'm older, I might change my mind. Right now I don't see myself having any children. It is just too much responsibility for me. I didn't want to give up my social life. I was just not ready at my age to have a child. I knew I would get an abortion.

I went to the clinic that my friend had told me about. I told the nurse I was pregnant. Then she did the urine test and told me I was about eight weeks pregnant. I didn't know I was that far along, I thought it was about a week or two. I told her that abortion is what I wanted to do. We discussed my option of going to a clinic or going to the hospital. In the clinic they don't totally knock you out, and it was out-of-state. I didn't want to be awake, I wanted to be knocked out. At the hospital you go right to sleep, plus it was downtown. I decided to go to the hospital. On this day my boyfriend was with me, but I made all the decisions myself.

I went to see the doctor who was going to do the abortion in about a week's time. That appointment wasn't scary, my boyfriend was with me. The doctor asked me if I was sure I wanted to do it. He asked me if I smoked and I said yes. He lectured me a little bit. I got instructions about when to be at the hospital, and about not having anything to eat after midnight before the operation, stuff like that. That week was scary. I don't like operations, I don't think anybody does. I didn't know what they were going to do to me.

During that week I was really paranoid that I was going to have a miscarriage, because I had heard all these horror stories from my friends. That would be too much shock for me. I was really cautious so I wouldn't have a miscarriage. I was still doing drugs, so I cut down, and also on cigarettes. People said, "Why? You're going to have an abortion." But I thought it wouldn't be right. Also, while I was pregnant and I was smoking up, it wasn't the same. It didn't feel the same. I felt paranoia, my heart would beat so fast. I had a bad stomach ache whenever I did it. I didn't like that.

A couple of days before I went to see this doctor, I called my mom. I said, "Hello, I'm pregnant." She freaked out. She said, "How could you be so irresponsible?" I told her I was having an abortion. She made me feel guilty about the pregnancy. She was lecturing me and yelling a bit. The reason I told her is because she was so open with me. She told me not to lie to her. I wanted to get along better with my parents. She told my dad. He didn't react how my mom did. He just told me, "Your mom told me you're pregnant. What are you going to do?" I said, "I'm going to have an abortion." I told them that I had gone to the clinic and that I had an appointment with the doctor. Whenever I saw them until after the

operation, the look on their faces was disappointment about the pregnancy. It made me feel sorry that I had disappointed them too.

After I went to the appointment, I told my mother when the abortion was going to happen. She still lectured me sometimes, but she offered to go with me. There was concern in her voice when she offered. I told her, "Mike is going to be there with me, so you don't have to." Plus one of my friends offered to come. I said, "If you really want to come, you can. But don't worry, I'll call you as soon as I get home." People were encouraging. My friends, my boyfriend, my parents, my sister, they all said, "You've made a good decision." I knew there were girls who were against it, but I didn't speak to them beforehand.

The night before, I was thinking, would I get up early enough to be on time, 'cause we were taking the bus over. I didn't sleep very well. I was happy that this was coming to an end and it was almost over.

When we got to the hospital, they took me into a locker-room where they had the hospital gowns, to get changed. The nurses were kind of bitchy. I had been waiting around, reading magazines, and I was getting nervous. When I went down to get the intravenous, Mike couldn't come with me, but he came later. The nurses were nicer, more calm. At first the nurse tried to do my IV but she couldn't. So I had to wait about twenty minutes, until the doctor who was going to do the operation did my IV. He was way nicer than the nurses, and that was a relief. After the IV they put a mask on me, and in a couple of minutes I was sleeping. While I was going under, I was trying to stay calm. I thought if I said anything, something might go wrong and I might die.

When I woke up I had abdominal pains, so I asked the nurse to give me some Tylenol. She gave it to me, then I said, "When am I going to see my boyfriend? I want to see my boyfriend." She said I have to wait twenty minutes, but it felt like an hour. Before I had the abortion, they gave me a paper saying what I should feel after, but I wasn't having a lot of the side-effects. They said I might feel depression, nausea, vomiting, cramping, bleeding. I was afraid they might all happen, but they didn't. I had some bleeding, but that's natural. I still had the abdominal pains. They were a little more uncomfortable than menstrual cramps. If you moved while you were lying down, it would hurt with the slightest movement. That went on for about two days. I stayed lying down for those two days.

I was really happy when I saw my boyfriend, and after that I was just happy. When Mike came in, he seemed a little worried about what I would tell him about how I was feeling. He said, "How are you?" I smiled and said, "Fine. I had some Tylenol and I feel fine." After he came in, I stayed for twenty minutes and then they gave me some cookies and apple juice. There was one nurse that was pleasant. The other nurses weren't really talking to me. They said I could leave if I wanted. I went to the locker-room and got changed. We took a taxi home.

When we got home, it was around noon. I felt really energetic. I watched TV for a while and fell asleep for about two hours. Then I had something light to eat, some mashed potatoes. I was happy that it was over and I didn't have to worry about it any more. Mike was sympathetic, offering to make me dinner, waiting on me. He was willing to do that. I called my mom before I went to sleep. She was happy. She said,

"Don't let it happen again." I called my dad and I told him everything went OK. He said, "Great." He was happy. I called my sister when she got home from school.

My mom was still lecturing me. I told her, "Mom, it happened. I can't do anything about it. But at least I'm smart enough not to bring a child into this world at my age, when I can't even support it." She said, "Yes, you're right." And she stopped after that.

After I got my period after the abortion, I went on the pill. It took about a week to get my period. A week after the operation I went back to the doctor for an appointment. He did an exam and he talked to me. I was less scared than I was for the first appointment.

At the hospital they told you not to have baths, have showers; for the bleeding, don't use tampons, use pads. So it was after a month that we had sex for the first time.

I wanted to, but I was a little scared about getting pregnant again and that it might hurt. Mike was begging me to. I said, "No, I can't. I have to wait a month." He said, "I can't wait a month." I said, "You're going to have to." I didn't feel flattered that he was so impatient. I thought he would be

more cautious. He knew before the abortion happened that we'd have to wait a month, but he was still begging me. I thought it was immature. He was acting like a regular guy: got to have it every day. I told him, "I thought you weren't like most guys. I thought you could live without it." He said, "I know, but I've waited for so long." Once it caused a fight, 'cause he was getting frustrated. After the abortion we had sex only once or twice a week. I was on the pill and using condoms all the time. After the abortion, we'd have a lot more fights.

I'm not living with him any more. I'm back living with my parents now. After about two months, I stopped thinking about the abortion, and forgot about it. I've never felt regret or guilty. Once in a while I would think that this was a good decision that I made. I haven't done any drugs since I was pregnant, and I'm in a career training program. When I was eighteen I dropped out of school. I want to go back now, to night school. I really want to go to college.

If I got pregnant tomorrow, I would still get an abortion. I wouldn't want that to happen, but I would still have an abortion. If I had a daughter and she told me she was pregnant, I would ask her what she would want to do. If she really wanted to have a kid, I wouldn't promote it. I would make her aware how much it is financially to have a kid, how much you spend on diapers and everything else. I would encourage adoption too. I was thinking about that for myself, but only for about two minutes. I didn't want to go through the physical pain of pregnancy.

Teenagers can have an abortion if they want to. They don't have to have kids. Teenage girls should really think about their choices.

Angela

tells her

STORY

I'm seventeen. My daughter will be one year old in two days. I lost my virginity when I was fourteen. He was my first boyfriend and I was in love with him. He never forced me or anything like that. It just happened. I just thought for some reason I wasn't going to get pregnant. Homer and I never really used birth control. When I was fourteen, I met up with a bunch of people who weren't exactly what you would call great people. I got mixed up in a lot of drugs, drinking almost every weekend, every day if I could, whenever money came in. It's not that my parents were easygoing, but they were hurt and I guess they just didn't know how to control me. My parents were very strict and they were very religious. My dad was really strict. So I wanted to rebel from that at the time. I don't know why. I didn't actually leave home, but I was never home. I usually stayed at Homer's place when I did

Angela arrived at the coffee shop early, anxious to tell me the adventures of being a seventeen-year-old mother. I knew who she was by the excitement in her eyes.

take off. I'd go back home, get some money, take a change of clothes with me. I dropped out of school and I was working.

Homer and I stayed together until I started realizing what the people we were hanging around with were doing. There were things in the newspaper every week that had something to do with my friends. They were in jail, Homer was in jail. I started getting disgusted. I wanted to get away from them. I wanted to leave. This took until I was fifteen. I decided that I'd changed and I wanted to be back with my family. That's when I found out I was pregnant.

I didn't want to believe it. I went and had a blood test. My doctor is really close with my family and I didn't want him to know, so I went to another doctor, in a walk-in clinic. She called me back and said I was pregnant. I was, I think, six to eight weeks pregnant. And I was living at home.

I called Homer and said I was pregnant. He didn't believe me. And he goes, "OK. Come to my house. I don't believe you." So I went to his house and we went through the story. I said, "I am, I am." And I just started crying. I said I was going to call my obstetrician. Then he sort of believed me. I guess he was shocked. Finally he says, "You're not keeping this baby." I didn't ever plan on having an abortion, even though I was poor. But I didn't know what to do. So I said, "No, I can't have an abortion. I can't do that. It's just me. I'm not saying anyone else shouldn't, but it's something within me, I couldn't do it." And then he switched. He said, "OK. I think I can get used to it."

I kept it a secret for a while. I wasn't big then, I didn't really show for a long time. I told my twin sister. She was the first person to know. She went to the doctor with me. She didn't persuade me, she just said she didn't think I should have an abortion. I never intended to have one. Friends, adults, pretty much everyone was telling me to get an abortion or give it up for adoption. But I couldn't do that. I figured, I did it, I'm the one who got pregnant, it's not the baby's fault that I'm pregnant.

My biggest fear about whether or not to have an abortion was my father. I just didn't know how to bring it up to him. I didn't know what he was going to do. I just knew I had to get out of my house. My first thought was, "He's going to kill me. He's going to beat the shit out of me." He'll just get so mad, yelling, screaming. He's not violent, but he can be. He has been. But not really that much to me. I was always my dad's favourite.

So I told my mom first. And my mom's first thing when she heard I was pregnant was to have an abortion right away. My mother told my father, later. I guess I would've been about four and a half months then. I was living at a pregnant girls' home. My mother had talked to some counsellor lady, who gave her the number of a home for pregnant girls and single mothers. My mother got flyers and stuff telling us what it is. So I said OK. The day my mother told my father, he called me at the home and started saying, "Oh they're rotten sperm. It's an evil thing. Why don't you have an abortion?"

At first I wanted to move out of my parents' home. I didn't want to live with my boyfriend because I don't like his family, they're sort of screwed up. They accept things that I wouldn't accept around my child. They were accepting his drugs, his drinking. Not even the drinking bothers me, but the drugs and stuff—I don't want that. I don't want it for my baby. So I wanted to get on my own, which I tried to do but I couldn't afford it.

I applied for assistance from welfare. That was the most humiliating thing, I think. It was just really low, you know. You have to go in there and practically beg them. I didn't think I should even be there. It's my fault; why should I get free money for things that I did? But I had to get money somehow. I went there and they gave me money. It was something like $400 a month.

I thought before that I was so mature, I could do anything I wanted. All of a sudden, when I got pregnant, it was like I was a little girl again. I would think, "I'm not capable of doing this. I don't have the maturity in my head to do this, to take care of a baby or to live on my own or budget my money. I don't want to even think about those things, but I have to." I just couldn't see myself on my own, so I went to the girls' home. And I was miserable. I lived there only for two weeks and then I came back home. My dad let me back home. I've been staying with my parents ever since.

The girls' home where I lived had a school. I went there up until a month before I had my baby, until I got really high blood pressure because I gained a lot of weight, so I couldn't go to school any more. I had to just stay off my feet. I got books. I read everything. I learned everything. I watched all kinds of programs. When you're pregnant, everything you think about is the baby. I really soaked up a lot of that stuff. It helped a lot. When Melony's sick, I know right away what's wrong. Half the time I'll go to the doctor's office and say she's got a rash, and I'll know what it is. So I learned a lot from school. I learned a lot from my friends, seeing them with their kids. I also learned from my mom. I had a lot of support from my mother.

I lost a lot of my friends. I guess they didn't know how to deal with me. I had no friends, I was totally ostracized. I was really depressed over that. Because I had no one. I mean, I would come home and have no one to talk to besides my mom and dad, my sisters and brothers. It's funny, when you need your friends the most—and that's one of the times when you do—you start acting differently. Everything changes. Your way of thinking changes. I have completely new friends now, that I'm just starting to get used to. Even if I see my old friends, it's not the same thing. We have nothing to talk about, it's like we just met. They've changed and I've changed. Well, they haven't changed, but I have. Not everybody's like that. A lot of my friends who have kids have kept their friends. But for some reason mine just flew. So I guess they weren't really my friends.

When you're first pregnant, you don't feel anything. I was in denial for a long time. Then, when it started to show, and the first time I felt it kick, I thought, "Wow!" It was amazing to feel something moving inside of me and know that I made that. I loved the feeling when the baby kicked. I liked being pregnant. My hair was a lot healthier, and my skin was really good. I liked my stomach, how it felt, how it looked in clothes. It's so comfortable when you're sleeping, you can rest your arm on your big stomach. The baby was huge, my stomach was really big. Everybody pays attention to you and wants to touch your stomach. It was a nice feeling, I still get flashbacks. I never had morning sickness, never threw up. It was a really good pregnancy.

I had a really long labour, three days. And the contractions were five minutes apart. I was really calm, but I was in very much pain. They gave me something to speed up my contractions, so I had to get an epidural, which I didn't want because it's not good for the baby. Then, when she was coming out, there were problems. Her head was turned the wrong way, her face was coming out first. So they had to turn her head around, and they couldn't do it. I remember for three, four hours I was pushing and nothing was happening. So they had this nut nurse come in. I couldn't feel my contractions and she kept telling me to push when my contractions came. So I kept getting really pissed off at this one nurse.

The nurses were horrible. I wanted to breast-feed. I tried to breast-feed, but I couldn't. And they were forcing me to do it. They wouldn't let me leave the hospital until I breast-fed. But I can't do it and the baby's screaming, starving. When you have this screaming child on your hands, what are you going to say—"You can't have any food until you breast-feed"? It doesn't understand. She just wanted to be calmed down. So I ended up bottle-feeding her, which I regret. I wish I would've tried harder.

When I found out I couldn't breast-feed, I started smoking again. I don't smoke around the baby. My brother and sister smoke a lot. I say, "Sorry, got to smoke outside," and they hate me for it. I'm not only her mother, but I also tell them what to do. So we all smoke outside. I don't want her to breathe that air.

I stopped drinking before I even knew I was pregnant. I realized I didn't like the people I was hanging around with and the things they were doing, so I stopped. I didn't do anything when I was pregnant, I'd feel guilty if I did. I smoked a little and I felt rotten when I did it. I just want to raise my baby saying, "You don't need that. You don't need to do drugs." So if I'm out there doing it, and then telling her she can't, she may look at me and say, "Who are you to tell me? You got pregnant when you were fifteen." That's my biggest fear. When she gets older, I'm going to tell her what I did was a mistake: "I should've been more prepared for you. I should've been able to give you more." Not her, she's not the mistake. What I did was a mistake.

When I was pregnant, my dad was really distant from me, which was really hard. I had an ultrasound which had the baby's picture on it. I tried to show it to him, but he didn't want to see it. He was really distant until the day my baby was born. And then my dad was like—even to this day he acts almost like the baby is his. He just goes nuts about Melony. And sometimes I think that's not good because I don't want Homer to think my father is taking over his place. My dad likes it if the baby calls him Dad. Which I don't mind, but then I think, how would my boyfriend feel? It hurts me a lot. No one in my family—no matter what they think about Melony's father—is allowed to talk about him, and they don't. I said I don't want the baby hearing things about her father. If they do talk about him, they'll say good things.

Staying with my parents is good in some ways and bad in other ways. Sometimes I think they're the ones who are raising her. They're like, "No, you can't have that, you shouldn't do this, or you shouldn't do that." And it really bothers me. Sometimes I feel like I don't have enough say. I don't feel Homer should, he's not there all the time. I take care of the baby twenty-four hours a day and he's there when he feels like it. I don't think he should have as much a say as I do, and probably not even as much as my parents.

I feel like Homer should be doing more somehow. I feel like we should be together as a family, that I shouldn't be with my parents. I think he takes them for granted. He knows the baby's not going to starve because my parents are there. It took Homer eighteen months to get a job and now he just finally started working. He gives me money, but he has a different way of looking at work. He gets his money from doing bad things, and I won't accept that. Sometimes I think I'm a bitch to him. Sometimes I'm hot in the head and I'll call him and harass him and say, "You need to do this and you need to do that." It only bothers me because of the baby. I'm not trying to change him, but there are certain things about him that I don't want my daughter to know. He's immature, I guess, but he's really changed a lot. He went out and got a job.

I'm happy with him, but I'm confused. I don't want to leave my parents' house. I just want my life to fall into place. It's hard. I'm getting money from welfare. They asked me about the father. Everybody told me not to tell them about him, but I'm not looking to rip off anything. So I said I knew him. They said I had to bring him into the office. When he was there, Homer said he wouldn't go on welfare. The lady said, "You're too good for assistance, but your daughter isn't?" They wanted me to take him to court. I said I'm not going to take him to court. They talked to him about how much money he has to give me. But I don't push him. I know when he has money he gives it to me. He is trying hard. When he has the money, he'll give me more than enough, he doesn't think two ways about it. He wants to see that his daughter has everything she needs.

Now he's starting to talk about moving in together. But I don't want to move in together, I want to get married. I don't think it's right just to live with him. I look at it like, "I'm good enough to sleep with you and I'm good enough to have your baby," and I feel like he just wants to stay with me until something more convenient comes along. So I want a commitment before I live with him. I want things to be stable. I'm not thinking of having these great jobs or anything, but just proper things.

I know I'm slamming my boyfriend. Actually, he's a lot better than some others. Some of my friends who have kids, the father is just gone. Homer's never done that. He's always stuck by me. I've nagged him for two years and he's stood by me. So he's a pretty good guy. He's my best friend. I know he loves me and I love him. Having Melony is better in some ways, because Homer and I love each other more and we know each other better.

My sex life has changed. I'm very insecure. I hate my body now. I feel fat, I feel disgusting. I'll tell that to Homer. He'll say, "I don't care what happened to you. I love you, it doesn't bother me." But it worries me. Every girl my age, they don't have kids and stretch marks. They can wear anything they want. My stomach has stretch marks all over it. I hope someday I'll get my body back. If I don't, I'll be sad, but that's the only thing.

I used birth control for a long time, but now we use condoms. When I was taking pills, there was something wrong. I kept getting blood clots, so I stopped taking them. Homer said he'll use condoms. But sometimes we get too far and then never get to use it. Now I'm paranoid about getting pregnant again. I don't want any more kids now.

I've changed a lot for the better. In some

ways it was better that I had her. And so did her father change a lot for the better. You know, the way we think, the way we do things—it's different now. When I had her, I knew I had to do something with my life. I couldn't just not worry about anything. I had to grow up. I had to start thinking about what I'm going to do with my future. If I could have waited I would have, because I lost out on a lot of things. You don't have, "What do I want to do today?" You lose that. You lose being able to go out whenever you want. I'm not saying it's bad. I wish I could be out there partying, but I can't now. Like before, I would go out and get plastered, then come back here and sleep all day. If I do that now, I know I'll be up at six in the morning, and I don't want to be cranky all day. I'll end up yelling at the baby. So I just want to make sure I can control myself and the things I do for my daughter's benefit. And it's good for me too.

I never would've been in school if it weren't for Melony. I went back to school because I know I don't want to be like other parents who can't make it. They don't even want to try. I'm in a special program 'cause I've been out of school for so long. It's called Rapid Path. I got sixteen credits for this year, which is pretty good. But I don't see my daughter all day, which feels bad. I feel I should be spending time with her, but it's also good in a way because it gives me a break, and it's good for her. It's hard having her all day long. You get cranky, you get upset. They're crying, you don't know what they want, you try to figure it out. But I do feel bad. I feel guilty about taking her to day care. If I had had her later on, I would have chosen to be with her.

My daughter's day care is subsidized, so I get it free. I felt really guilty about taking her to day care, but I find that she learns faster there because there are other kids and she's learning from them. She really likes it. She gets excited when she gets there, starts shaking her arms and stuff. She's more sociable. When she goes out and sees people, she'll smile at them. She's not scared of anyone. She's really loving, so it helps her a lot. She's never going to get bored at day care. There is always something that she's doing and she has fun there. I have more energy to take care of her when I get her after school because I've had my break.

But just recently, she started crying when I drop her off. I don't know what to do, I just feel so bad. You have this baby grabbing on your leg. It's hard to walk out of there knowing she doesn't want you to leave. I look at her little face and I know she doesn't know when I'm going to come back.

I want to make sure I have a good job so that my baby has things she wants and I can take care of her better. That's why I'm stuck in this position. Like when I don't have money and stuff, my parents are always there, I can fall back on them. I know it's probably not right that I have them to fall back on. I wish I had more money. For some reason money is the answer to me now. I need money, money, money, 'cause there's never enough. I want some sort of stability. I feel trapped that way. I could leave my parents' house, but what with? I have no furniture. I couldn't have extras like I have now. If I want to go out and buy something today, if I was on my own, I couldn't do that.

I never asked my parents to do anything for me, but they do it. They never complain or say anything, and sometimes maybe I take it for granted a little bit. I pay my parents $300 a month for rent. My income is $449 and you can't live off it, there is no way. I usually take care of all of Melony's food and diapers. I buy most of her clothes. Homer buys a lot of stuff, he bought her shoes for winter. I'm not greedy with myself, I'll go without, but I'll buy everything for her. My parents help me out a lot. If I go out and overspend, they'll fix it up for me. At first I liked it, but I don't like it any more. Now I want to be independent, I want to learn how to do things myself. That's what I'm trying to do. I'm starting to get furniture, to get things. I'm starting to actually think, "Gee! I have a family." It's finally hit me, I guess. So now I'm starting to mature a little, bit by little bit.

You know what would make me happy right now? My own house, peace and quiet, not my brothers and sisters and everybody in this small little house. I would like to be married to my baby's father. Just me, him and our baby—that's what I want. I'm hoping Homer's going to get there someday. I know he's kind of slow. But I'm happy in some ways. Nobody has exactly what they need. And that's just the way it is. You can't change it. Things work out. They all fall into place somehow. I know that will happen, with or without money. Just—money would be nice.

I have friends who have kids. You always get everybody's advice. You'll have your mother and grandmother and all these people giving you advice you don't want, and you just kind of sit there and go, "Sure..." They'll always be there to tell you what to do. The only thing I wish I would've known is that babies stay up half the night and you don't get any sleep. That's what I wasn't prepared for, that hit me the most, not sleeping. I'd sleep maybe half an hour in twenty-four hours. She'd be up constantly, all night long.

Six a.m. is when I usually wake up. My mom will feed Melony while I take my shower, then she'll bring her in and we'll take a shower together. I like it that she takes a shower with me, so we spend time together before she goes off to day care and I go off to school. I get her ready and my mom helps, and my dad will play with her while I get dressed. My dad usually drives us. He'll drop the baby off then drop me off at school, which is really nice. I pick her up after school, by four-thirty.

The whole family cooks, but just me and my baby eat together. As long as she's in the highchair I have to eat, 'cause as soon as she's out of it, you have to chase her around the house. Then we'll go in and watch TV or I'll play with her on the floor. I like to play with her 'cause I've been away the whole day. She likes to dance, I always dance with her. She loves my dad, so when he comes home she gets really excited. My whole family helps out and plays with her, so it's good. She's in a really loving environment. Then I give her her bath. Everyone will come in and watch. Then I get her dressed and comfortable. I rock her, or my mother will rock her, she likes that. Melony's really affectionate and I'm like that too. She's a really good baby, really happy, never really cranky.

I try to get her to sleep by eight-thirty, which you can't really do. I don't care what anybody says. You have to have a routine, but I don't believe there's such a thing. Everything is rushed, it's never relaxed. Even when you're relaxing, you're thinking that she's going to be up any minute, I got to hurry up and do this or that. The best time is when we play together, because nobody's rushed about that. I have all the time in the world to play with her and I'm not thinking about anything else.

Eventually she goes to sleep. Then I do my homework if I

have any. Then I'll call her dad and fill him in on what the baby did for the day if he hasn't seen her. I talk to her father every day or I'll get the baby to talk to him. I know he feels bad that he can't be there. My father won't let him in the house, he says he doesn't want him here. It hurts me a lot that he's not allowed there. I feel hurt for Homer more than I feel hurt for myself and for my daughter. My mother and every-one in my family accepts him, except for my dad. But he's starting to come around. Eventually I hope he lets Homer in.

Melony likes her dad. Her dad has more energy than me and will take her everywhere and do all kinds of stuff. He's scared to take the baby on his own. I don't know why, maybe it's just an excuse. I'll say, "I need to go out, I'm going insane." Then he'll say, "OK, come over and drop the baby off and you can go out." When I go over, he'll end up saying, "You have to come here and spend some time with me too." He wants me to live with him, but I don't want to. Maybe I'm being stubborn. I told him, it's for Melony's benefit. When it's time for me to leave the nest, even if it's just me and my daughter, at least Homer can come over and if I tell him to leave, he has to leave.

To be honest, my daughter is more stable where I am right now because she has a lot of love and everything she needs. I know if I run out of money, she'll have something to fall back on. If I was living on my own—I don't know, I've never tried it. It's not that I can't do it, I'm just scared to try.

When my friends say, "I really want a baby," I'll say to them, "Don't get pregnant. Come over to my house at four a.m. and play with my baby, but don't have a baby." Before I got pregnant, I thought it would be fun. I have a lot of support and it's still hard.

■

I'm doing this interview because, when I was pregnant and going to school, I remember going to the library looking for books on young people having children, and there was nothing. I thought people should write books on this stuff, something that we could relate to. All the books were, "Your husband..." and my prenatal classes were, "You and your husband..." When I went to prenatal class, I just had myself and I'd feel like an idiot. There was never anything on young people. Some people say they care, but then why isn't there stuff about it out there? You know why? It's because we're looked down upon. Even though times have changed, I walk around the streets with my daughter and people will still look at me like, "Look at that little slut." That's just how people are, so it's good to tell people not to do that.

If some people want to have kids, it's not the worst thing that could happen. It's good to hear other people's stories, that you're not the only one, you're not alone. It's good for people to hear that I'm glad to have my daughter, and also good to hear negative things that can happen. The only reason I kept her is because I had my family. Some people don't have anybody, and welfare is just not enough, so they have to give the baby up for adoption, even abortion. I couldn't do it, it is just my personal thing. I think about what I'm doing, but some people don't, they just keep doing it. It's a really important issue.

You are pregnant — now what?

By Katherine A. Kelly, R.N., B.S.N., C.E.N.
Rideout Memorial Hospital, Marysville, California

Dealing with the Initial Shock*

You are sitting in the office of the doctor who has cared for you for many years, or, wanting anonymity, you have gone to someone you've never met. It seems like you have been there forever and you just want to go home and hide from the world. The problem is, you also desperately want to know the answer to the ultimate question: are you pregnant? You sit there, hoping and trying to reassure yourself that it's just some fluke of nature that you haven't had a period for three months. The doctor walks in, looks at you and tells you that you are eight weeks pregnant. Your heart jumps to your throat, your stomach churns and you begin to shake all over. Maybe you feel like your whole life is over, but at the same time there might be positive feelings as well. You look down at your stomach and back at the doctor with dozens of questions in your head. Where do you start?

The doctor starts talking about your options, appointments, ultrasounds, health insurance and so on. You don't hear a word because you are immediately worried about what you are going to tell your family and friends and how they will react. You might suddenly feel very alone in the world. As you make your way home, your mind races through the obvious options: you could hide the pregnancy from everyone (but for how long?), or get an abortion immediately (but how and by whom, and how do you pay for it?).

If you were raped or are the victim of incest, call an emergency crisis line or clinic right away—they have the best resources to help you.

You have just been through one of the most stressful experiences a woman can have. You are faced with hundreds of issues about your life and your pregnancy. The issues are complicated and charged with emotion.

You can take one of two pathways in handling this situation. One, you can allow people around you to take over your life and get you through this with very little input from you. This would allow them to make decisions that you will have to live with, and possibly regret. (see Getting Help, below). This might be a way of avoiding conflict and pressure, but in the long run it may not make you very happy.

Two, you can work towards taking charge of your life in a way that you may never have done before. This will take a lot of strength and courage. It might not be easy. The payoff is that you will make decisions that—as much as possible—will meet your needs rather than other people's. They will be decisions that you feel you can live with. You will gradually feel stronger and have better self-esteem as a result of learning to take control: the more you do it the more you will have. Also, if you decide to continue with your pregnancy, making your own choices will probably give your child the best chance for happiness.

Getting Help—the Next Step

First, you need to get reliable information, and as soon as possible. Once you have decided whether you will continue with your pregnancy, you will have to act quickly, but right now you need to give yourself time to think and to get the best information available to help you make your choice. There are several ways to do this. The telephone book is an excellent place to start. An organization called Planned Parenthood has offices in many communities and offers cost-free, valuable information and counselling services. Some branches have health-care professionals who will do most tests and examinations for free. Women's clinics and crisis clinics are also good places to call. There are other organizations and clinics listed that offer counselling for pregnant teens, but evaluate these carefully. Some of them have hidden biases and try to persuade teens to make one particular kind of decision about their pregnancy. It is extremely important that you keep this fact in mind: nobody should give you advice about which choice to make. If you are talking to someone who makes you feel guilty or pressured, or even just uncomfortable, find another organization. Libraries and women's bookstores have information on local clinics and counselling services too.

Another source of information might be your school nurse or family doctor. You should be aware, though, that even health-care professionals sometimes have unsympathetic reactions to pregnant teenagers and might be unsupportive. Try not to let this upset you too much. These attitudes are their problem, and should not be made into yours as well.

Dealing with Negative Attitudes

Unfortunately, you will be treated with negativity or hostility by some people. When people pass judgement on you, remind yourself that you're not a bad person, you're just pregnant. And it's your pregnancy, not theirs. Try to be strong and show courage. Even your friends might have an unexpected reaction to you, which can be especially hard. If any of these people upset you, talk about your feelings with family or friends who are supportive of you, or talk to your counsellor. Try to spend time with these understanding people instead. After a while you will find yourself learning new coping skills for difficult situations.

Examining Your Options

Making your decision will be extremely emotional. At the same time, it is one that should be made with intelligence and a full understanding of the consequences. It requires you to take into consideration the plans you have for your own life. If you possibly can, try to get some counselling from a professional health-care worker (like a doctor or nurse), clinic or public health organization. They will give you information and talk with you about each of your options: abortion, adoption or motherhood.

It is important to remember that it's natural to have second thoughts, whatever your final decision. This is a very complicated choice to make, and many teens feel insecure or confused if they have mixed feelings. Don't expect a perfect decision from yourself; there is no such thing. If you have carefully thought through your choice, you will probably identify it as the best choice possible for you under the circumstances.

1. Ending your pregnancy: An abortion is a medical procedure that must be done under sterile conditions, usually in a hospital or clinic. Go to a responsible health-care professional, clinic or health organization that will offer you counselling and proper care. If they do not perform abortions themselves, they can put you in contact with a clinic or doctor that does.

Ask for an appointment to visit the clinic and meet the staff. Your appointment will be completely private, and no one will tell your parents. Ask all the questions in your mind—it is the staff's job to help you understand everything you need to know before making your decision.

2. Choosing adoption: Clinics and Planned Parenthood organizations can help you with information, which can get complicated because adoption laws are very different from country to country and region to region. Make every effort to understand the laws in your area. Sometimes, placing your child for adoption can be done in very creative ways so as to allow you to continue to have some contact with the child.

Regardless of all the practical reasons for choosing abortion or adoption, the emotional issues may override all of them. These emotions are among the strongest you will feel in your entire life, and they will not end with abortion or adoption. Ask your doctor or clinic to put you in touch with support groups that can help you deal with the feelings you may have when this is all over.

3. Keeping the baby: When you consider this option, it's important that you talk to your family, the father of the baby (if possible), and anyone else who would be closely involved in your life once the baby is born. Make sure you find out what kind of support, emotional and financial, you could expect from them. Talk to a school counsellor to find out what sort of arrangements you might be able to make about your education, both now and in the future.

If you choose to keep the baby, you need to get proper health care. This is your responsibility towards yourself and your child. Find a good doctor right away. A family doctor, or GP, is a good place to begin. In addition, there are mid-level practitioners who can offer excellent care during your pregnancy. Ask your clinic or counsellor for more information about these health-care workers.

Teenage pregnancies can be prone to complications because of your age. Make a list of questions for your health-care professional about how to look after yourself during your pregnancy. Ask about activity, eating habits, smoking, drugs and alcohol consumption. Ask about reading materials, getting appointments and tests. If your partner is supportive and wants to be involved in the process, this is a good time to include him. Get started in birthing and parenting classes as soon as you can. If possible, these should be done together with your partner. Ask your counsellor or doctor about special classes for teenagers. Keep in contact with your health-care worker, keep your appointments and pay attention to their recommendations: they are very important and will ultimately determine the health of you and your child.

Money

If you live in the United States and money for medical or counselling services is a problem, contact local government agencies such as Aid for Dependent Children. There are also Medicaid programs available to pregnant women of all ages; for information about these, call your local Health Department or the Department of Social Services. (These organizations sometimes have names different from these. To find out more, phone the operator or ask at your local library.)

In Canada, counselling services are offered free of charge at teen clinics in hospitals. If there is no teen clinic in your area, contact Planned Parenthood. Medical services performed in hospitals are covered by government health plans. Private clinics do charge fees, though they may waive the charge or ask you to pay what you can. Be sure to check in advance to determine what financial arrangements can be made.

What Do I Tell My Parents?

This might depend partly on what decision you make about your pregnancy. Some teens who choose abortion decide not to tell their parents, fearing a hostile reaction.

If you decide to tell them about your pregnancy, try to think through ahead of time what you want to say and what the facts are. Talk it over with someone you trust, whether a friend, counsellor, spiritual leader, partner or someone else. If you are especially nervous, it might be a good idea to have another person with you, someone who is sympathetic to you and can offer you support during the family discussion. Ask that person ahead of time, tell them what you want to talk about and give them time to decide. If one person says no, don't get discouraged—find another one. Some organizations offer counselling services involving parents. There may be a health-care professional, teacher or sports coach who would be willing to be present when you talk to your parents.

Your parents might not react the way you expect—positively or negatively. You might be nervous, but what you don't need to be is ashamed. You have not committed a crime. What has happened has happened and cannot be reversed; therefore, it is important to move on and make decisions about the future.

Your parents might want to dwell on the "horrible mistake you've made," they might want to say "I told you so." They might feel that it's their right to make the decisions, to control you and the situation. Quite simply, it is not. Your parents' decisions might be based on their need to save face or avoid the neighbours finding out. Remember that, while they might be suffering some embarrassment, you are facing a life-changing event. The consequences are yours alone. Don't misunderstand: your parents are not the villains here, but they have a very different point of view than you do at this time.

Take this time to try and take control of your choices and future. Let your family know that you have given some thought to your options. If possible, involve your partner in this effort.

Coping with Stress

This is, of course, a very stressful time for you, but there are some basic steps that can help you deal with it.

1. Don't make big decisions right away. You are not yet in the frame of mind to think clearly through many of the decisions you will have to make. Make only the simpler ones at this point: choosing what doctor you are going to see, which person or people you want to confide in initially, and so on. (These might not seem like simple decisions, but they are as simple as they get in this situation.) Keep in mind, however, that the decision to end your pregnancy ideally should be made before the twelfth week. Abortions that are done after that point are more complicated.

2. Find a friend. Someone might surface in your life as your much-needed friend. It might not be who you think it will be. They may not always know what to say or do, but they do want to help. Try not to shut people out because they don't understand what you're going through. Explaining what is happening to you could help them understand, and it might give you a chance to gain new perspectives on things.

3. If possible, talk with the father. Find out what you can expect from him. Let him know that what you need right now is emotional support. Just like you, he is going to find this a very confusing and difficult time. You may need to give him some time to think clearly and offer you the support you need. Don't expect it to happen immediately: it might take a while or, in some cases, never happen at all.

A man's view of pregnancy is very different from a woman's. His priorities are very different from yours. He is not influenced by the same pressures and emotions that you are in this situation, and he may see things in a strictly practical way. He might, for example, arrive at the idea of abortion before you do. He might feel that this is the only answer at first, and it does not necessarily mean that he doesn't care about you or wants to "get rid of the baby." Explore with him why he feels the way he does and try to understand it. Again, keep in mind that it is your body and ultimately your decision.

Many of us as teenagers have a very hopeful view of our prospects for marriage and family life, even if our family life was far from perfect. Because of this, you might decide that you ought to get married. However, now is not the time to make that decision; it is a big one, and you and your partner need to make it without pregnancy being a factor. Don't pressure him to get married, and resist your parents' pressure as well.

4. Try to avoid confrontations. Talking with friends and relatives may lead to uncomfortable discussions that bring up or intensify long-standing problems in those relationships. If you feel that this is happening, try to get out of the conversation and avoid that person in future. Become aware of people who put pressure on you or try to control you, and of situations that are uncomfortable in these ways. Avoid them if you can. You might also find counselling helpful in learning coping skills for these and other situations that you may find yourself in.

5. Try to stay on course. The fact that you are pregnant doesn't mean that you have to give up all of your dreams for the future. If anything, you need to become more committed to those dreams. You may have to deal with some delays and/or find another route to achieve your goals, but you are young. You have the strength and courage to achieve them. Avoid any decision that closes doors to opportunities. For example, don't turn down scholarships or admissions to colleges or universities; these things can be postponed for a variety of reasons, and pregnancy can be one of them.

Learning and Growing

Everything in your life has changed, and change can be hard to accept. You might feel older, or find that things that were once very important to you don't somehow seem that important any more. One day you may look around at your friends and suddenly think they seem very young. It may be hard to fit in with your usual friends.

The way you view your parents will change. Your relationship with your partner will undoubtedly change—or might even end. These are things over which you may not have control.

However, you can work on controlling your responses. Try to focus on the aspects that are positive. Perhaps you have found a new friend who understands what you are going through. You might even find that you and your parents become closer. New dreams, just as exciting and fulfilling, might replace the old ones.

Believe in yourself. Because of all you are going through, you are going to grow and learn. You are going to find within yourself more strength than you ever thought possible. Recognize these resources within yourself and take pride in your ability to draw on them.

Nothing in life can give you more satisfaction than making your own choices and finding within yourself the courage to see them through.